Jonathan Blake

History of the Town of Warwick, Massachusetts

From its First Settlement to 1854

Jonathan Blake

History of the Town of Warwick, Massachusetts
From its First Settlement to 1854

ISBN/EAN: 9783743408500

Manufactured in Europe, USA, Canada, Australia, Japa

Cover: Foto ©ninafisch / pixelio.de

Manufactured and distributed by brebook publishing software (www.brebook.com)

Jonathan Blake

History of the Town of Warwick, Massachusetts

HISTORY

OF THE

TOWN OF WARWICK,

MASSACHUSETTS,

FROM ITS FIRST SETTLEMENT TO 1854.

BY

HON. JONATHAN BLAKE.

BROUGHT DOWN TO THE PRESENT TIME BY OTHERS.

WITH AN APPENDIX.

BOSTON:
NOYES, HOLMES, AND COMPANY,
219 WASHINGTON STREET.
1873.

PREFACE.

THE following brief outline of the early history of the town of Warwick, Mass., by the Hon. Jonathan Blake, was written about forty years ago, in 1831 and 1832. A small part of it has been written since that time. It was compiled from the most authentic records of the town, made at the time when the various transactions took place; and it contains matters of deep and thrilling interest to all the inhabitants, whether they be the regular descendants of the first inhabitants or not. All naturally wish to know something of the origin, character, and condition of the first settlers,—of those who first opened their eyes on this beautiful landscape, this wild mountain scenery, this Switzerland of America; and here pitched their tents, on these sloping hill-sides and in these winding valleys, beside the running streams, and babbling brooks, and quiet ponds, surrounded by the tall pines of the forest. All wish to know something of the hardy pioneers, who felled the giant trees, cleared up these cultivated fields, made these roads, built these walls, erected these houses, and did so much for the comfort and accommodation of the present inhabitants. To all, then, who have come into possession of this goodly inheritance, it contains matters of great and absorbing interest, which ought to be preserved for future generations. Without any view to publication, it was written expressly for the Warwick Lyceum, before whom select portions of it were read, at different times, as lyceum lectures, to the great edification of the hearers. It was not designed to give a full or complete account even, of the early history of Warwick, but only so much of it as would be interesting to the members of the lyceum; and even now it is not thought advisable by the publishing committee to enlarge upon this branch of the subject by attempting to supply what may have been omitted.

From this brief outline, however, we have something more than a glimpse, or a mere bird's-eye view, of our forefathers. We have a tolerably correct account of their characters and habits, their spirit and enterprise, their sayings and doings, their joys and rejoicings, their trials and hardships, their privations and sufferings, and their noble devotion to the cause of education, religion, and good government. The work is now printed just as it was left by its venerated author, and transcribed by his brother, Samuel Blake, both of whom are now numbered with the sainted dead.

The committee of publication were requested to write out and complete the history, so well begun by Mr. Blake, and to bring it down to the present time. This, at first, the committee thought could not be well done without making it appear like patchwork, —like new cloth on an old garment. But, after a little reflection upon the subject, they concluded to make the attempt, and to do the best they could to complete the work, and to make it match with the early history of the town. From the town-records and other authentic sources, they have collected all the facts and materials they have used in completing the work. With what success they have executed it, each one must judge for himself. Though the whole committee have given their general approbation to all that has been added, without being able to certify to the truth of every particular fact or statement, yet each member is particularly responsible for the articles which stand over the initials of his name.

It is hoped the book will be acceptable to all. By all the *natives* of the town, whether living here or elsewhere, it will be regarded with high favor, as a kind of godsend, or heirloom, to remind them of their father and mothers, their brothers and sisters, their kindred and friends. And to all *others* it will show

how strong, in the breasts of all the natives of Warwick, are the veneration and love of their birthplace, and the home of their childhood. What shrine is more sacred, what spot is more holy, than the place of one's nativity? J. G.

WARWICK, March 4, 1872.

INSTRUCTIONS TO THE COMMITTEE.

WARWICK, Dec. 26, 1871.

At a meeting of the citizens of the town, held at the Centre Schoolhouse, for the purpose of considering the propriety of securing the publication of the Hon. Jonathan Blake's "History of Warwick," and of taking measures for the furtherance of said object, —

Voted, and chose Hervey Barber, Chairman; Edward F. Mayo, Secretary; Hervey Barber, John Goldsbury, Nahum Jones, S. P. French, and E. F. Mayo, a Committee to take the matter into consideration, and adopt such measures as they may deem expedient to accomplish the purpose.

Voted, To adjourn to the call of the committee.

Jan. 3, 1872. — The committee met according to appointment, and passed the following measures as necessary for the purpose of accomplishing the trust committed to their charge: —

Resolved, That it is the sense of this committee that Blake's "History of Warwick" be brought down to the present time.

Voted, That the Rev. John Goldsbury and Deacon Hervey Barber be requested to take the matter in charge, bring the work down to the present time, and prepare the same for publication.

Voted, To adjourn without day.

EDWARD F. MAYO,
Secretary.

INSTRUCTIONS TO THE COMMITTEE.

Article 19th of the Annual March Meeting was as follows: To see if the town will take any action in regard to the publication of Blake's "History of Warwick," and appropriate money for the same.

March 4, 1872, on Article 19th, *Voted*, That the committee be authorized to borrow money for the purpose.

A. S. ATHERTON,
Town Clerk.

HISTORY OF WARWICK, MASS.

THERE is a trait inherent in the character of man which is common to us all, — every one more or less feels its influence ; and that is a wish and a desire to look into futurity, — to see and to know what is laid up for us in the vast storehouse (if I may be allowed the expression) of coming events. And equally curious, and equally careful, are we all to explore the past, to investigate, to search out, from whence we came, and where we originated. The creation of the world, the creation of man and every living thing that exists, whether material or immaterial, are the constant subjects of our inquiry. And it is just the same with regard to inanimate nature : the busy and inquisitive mind of man, with eagerness and assiduity, searches out the past, the present, and the future ; and, where the faithful page of history is wanting, conjecture and imagination

NOTE. — This was written for the amusement and information of the Warwick Lyceum, at several different times, in 1831 and 1832, by Jonathan Blake, jun. Copied from the original manuscript by Samuel Blake.

supply the deficiency. With what an intense interest do we seek and inquire after the ruins of Pompeii, buried for such a lapse of ages from human inspection by the eruption of Mount Vesuvius, that the memorial of the transaction was almost lost to the world! The meanest articles of domestic use that were in vogue in those ancient times are more valued by us, and excite greater admiration, than the most costly furniture in modern use. The brilliant and successful achievements of ˙Champollion in deciphering the hieroglyphics on the monuments and temples, and in the tombs, of Egypt, excite our wonder, and fill us with surprise; and we catch at every word and sentence that will throw light on the history of centuries that have long since rolled away.

The first settlement of this country by Europeans has now become interesting by the lapse of only about two hundred years; and we lament the inattention and neglect of our forefathers in not recording the facts and circumstances of the times in which they lived: many events are already lost to the present age and to posterity forever. But let us rescue from oblivion what now remains: let us faithfully record every thing that our fathers have done within our knowledge, and hand it down to our children. They will be grateful, they will feel thankful, for the historical legacy bequeathed to them by those that have gone before them. The uncivilized natives of this country have set us an example: they hand down from father to son what we can more accurately and more faithfully preserve by our superior knowledge, and acquaintance with letters.

The theme of our inquiry now is the history of Warwick; and, although but sixty-eight years have passed away since it was incorporated as a town, many of us could give but a very imperfect account of the scenes that have transpired, and none of us can do justice to the subject. Scarcely three ages have elapsed since this spot * on which we are now convened, and all the adjacent hills and dales, were a howling wilderness, — no trace of improvement, not a vestige of the works of art, not a lonely cultivated field, not a solitary dwelling for civilized man; but, on the contrary, the whole surrounding country was covered, far and wide, with an almost impenetrable and illimitable forest. The mind unaccustomed to reflection, and unacquainted with woods and wilds, can have but a faint idea of the solitude and gloom of a boundless wilderness; and those that reflect and consider, and fancy to themselves that they can realize how it looked, how it appeared, and how it was, here "in olden time," may all be mistaken. A sullen gloom, a death-like silence, pervaded the land. Now and then, perhaps, a wandering native might traverse these iron-bound hills in the pursuit of game, or in quest of his enemies. But the prowling beasts of prey and the feathered tribes were the only permanent settlers in these then desolate regions. But, gloomy and silent and desolate as it was, it was destined by the great Author of our existence to be the residence of man; and, had it not been a wilderness covered with timber, man could not have subsisted here. We are

* The schoolhouse on the common, in the middle of the town.

indebted to this wonderful display of Infinite wisdom for all the means of enjoyment, and all the various blessings, which we now enjoy. In an inland country like ours, where, nearly one-half of the year, the water is congealed to ice, and the ground covered with snow, the ingenuity of man has not yet discovered the means of sustaining human beings without the aid of wood and timber ; and at this moment, had not wood and timber been found here, these mountains and hills and plains would have been as devoid of the habitations of man as the arid and scorched plains of Africa, or the vast and extensive wastes in the open country beyond the Mississippi and the Rocky Mountains.

But to return to the subject. In the year 1735, June 10, "at a great and general court or assembly for his Majestic's Province in the Massachusetts Bay," in answer to the petitions of Samuel Newall, Thomas Tileston, Samuel Gallop, and Abraham Tilton, and others in connection with each of them, the said court voted "that four several tracts of land for townships, each of the content of six miles square, be laid out in suitable places in the western parts of this province ; and that the whole of each town be laid out into sixty-three equal shares, one share of which to be for the first settled minister, one for the use of the ministry, and one for schools ; and that, on the other sixty shares in each town, there be sixty settlers admitted, and, in the admission thereof, preference to be given to the petitioners, and such as are the descendants of the officers and souldiers who served in the expedition to Canada, in the year 1690" (viz., one of the said townships to each of the aforesaid persons, with such others as joined with them in the petitions) ; "and in case there be not a sufficient number named in the said four petitions as were either officers or souldiers in the said expedition, or the descendants of such as were lost, or are since deceased, so as to make sixty settlers for each town, that then such others as were in the expedition, or their descendants, be admitted settlers there, until sixty persons in each township be admitted ; and inasmuch as the officers and souldiers in that expedition were very great sufferers, and underwent uncommon hardships, *Voted*, That this Province be at the sole charge of laying (out) the said four townships, and of admitting the settlers. That the settlers or grantees be, and hereby are, obliged to bring forward the settlements of the said four townships in as regular and defencible a manner as the situation and circumstances will admit of, — and that in the following manner (viz.) : that they be on the granted premises respectively, and have each of them an house eighteen feet square, and seven feet stud, at the least ; that each right or grant have six acres of land brought to, and ploughed or brought to English grass, and fitted for mowing ; that they respectively settle in each plantation or township a learned orthodox minister, and build a convenient meeting-house for the public worship of God in each township."

These conditions to be complied with within five years from the confirmation of the Platts. Committees were appointed to lay out the aforesaid grants ; and bonds were required of each settler, under the penalty of twenty pounds running to the treasurer of the Province ; and if the grantees, or any of the grantees, fail of fulfilling the terms aforesaid, they forfeited all their title back to the Province.

Warwick was one of these four grants, and the one petitioned for by Samuel Newall and others; and it was at first called the plantation of "*Roxbury, or Gardner's Canada.*"

In June, 1736, Samuel Newall, and the officers and soldiers in the company, under the command of Capt. Andrew Gardner in the Canada expedition, were authorized by the General Court to call their first meeting of the proprietors. Said meeting was held at the house of James Jarvis, in Roxbury, Sept. 22, 1736. Capt. Robert Sharp was chosen moderator, and William Dudley, Esq., proprietors' clerk.

At this meeting, a committee, consisting of Capt. Robert Sharp, Ensign Samuel Davis, and Mr. Gershom Davis, was chosen to procure a surveyor, and lay out the "home lots." Each lot to contain not less than fifty acres, nor more than sixty acres; and each proprietor was taxed twenty-three shillings to defray the expense of laying out said lots, and paying the costs incurred in petitioning the court, &c.

It is not now known at what time these home lots were laid out; but by the proprietors' records, on the 24th of October, 1737, the sixty proprietors by name drew for their respective lots, and paid twenty shillings each to defray the expense. The home lots, as they are called, began to be numbered in the south-west part of the town, and were laid one hundred and sixty rods long, and fifty rods wide. Mr. Henry Fuller owns the largest part of lot No. 1; and the stones are now visible where they built their first camp, previous to surveying these lots.

These lots continue on to the north part of Chestnut Hill; then several of them were located south of the meeting-house, where Mr. Elijah Fisk now lives; then north of the meeting-house, and over the hill to Medad Pomroy's; then, beginning at Mr. James Ball's, they continue on to near the north line of the town.

Thus you see that they selected the hills, or high ridges of land, for the first settlements; and this is one reason why almost all our roads were located over the hills, instead of passing through the valleys.

The boundaries of Warwick, as it was originally laid out, were as follows: on the west line by Northfield, six miles and thirty-eight rods; then on Erving's Grant, two miles and thirty-nine rods; making whole west line eight miles and seventy-seven rods. North, on the line of New Hampshire, four miles and ninety-eight rods on the town of Winchester, and two miles and forty-two rods on the town of Richmond; making the whole north line six miles and one hundred and forty rods (it was originally called Arlington and Province land, north). East, on Province land (now Royalston) and Pequeag (Athol), on Province land six miles and thirty rods;* thence, west one hundred and seventy-nine rods to the north-west corner of Pequeag; thence, south two hundred and fifty-six rods to a heap of stones on the west line of Pequeag, and to a small maple-tree south on Erving's Grant, four miles and two hundred and sixty-five rods.

---

* Allowing one rod in thirty for sag of chain, as the old records say was customary.

The west and north boundaries of Warwick continue the same as originally laid out; but when the town of Orange was incorporated, which took off the south-east corner, it left the east line on Royalston three miles and one hundred and two rods; the south line, two miles and one hundred and eighteen rods; and the south-east is a zig-zag line, measuring five miles and three hundred and sixteen rods on the town of Orange.

It contained twenty-three thousand acres of land, exclusive of the Great Farm (so called), which was a grant previously made of sixteen hundred acres to one Johnson and his company, for military services; and is the land that Mr. Aaron Bass, Samuel Williams, Parley Leland, Samuel Fay, Samuel Moore, and others, now own; and also exclusive of the Severance and Field Farms. The Severance Farm contained two hundred acres, on which Jonathan Blake, and Jonathan Blake, jun., Bunyan Penniman, Asa Ware, and Stephen Ball, now live, and each of them owns a part of it. It is a traditional story, that it was granted as a reward for the faithful services of the surveyor who laid out this part of the country, and that he had his choice to select where he pleased. The Field Farm never belonged to Warwick, but made a notch in the south-east corner. It contained four hundred acres; and Deacon Ward and Jessie Warrick now live on a part of it.

Late in the fall of 1737, a second division of lots was laid out under the direction of a committee, consisting of Deacon Davis and Ebenezer Case, who were empowered " to agree with one or more surveyors and chain-men and pilots." These second-division lots were called farms, and were to contain one hundred and fifty acres each, if the land would hold out: and the surveyors were directed to qualify them; viz, to lay them out according to the quality of the land, — the poorest land into the largest lots, and the best into smaller ones, so as to have them valued alike. This is the reason why the second-division lots are so unequal in size, varying from one to two hundred acres: for instance, on " Beech Hill" the old original lots contain but about one hundred acres each, that being considered the best of the land; while the broken lots contain nearly or quite two hundred.

I have had occasion to mention sectional and local names in different parts of the town, some of which remain, while others are lost or forgotten. It may not be amiss to state these names for the information of those that may come after us, with the origin, or probable origin, of the same. "Beech Hill," above mentioned, lies in the east part of the town, where Mr. Abijah Eddy and Mr. Calvin Allen now live; and the name originated from the large and uncommon growth of beech timber it formerly contained. "Chestnut Hill" was so named for the same reason, the chestnut-trees being the most common growth. It is located in the south-west part of the town, where the Messrs. Francis and Jonas Leonard, Joseph Wilson, and Capt. William Burnett, and others, now reside. "Flour Hill" is in the north part of the town, where Messrs. Phinehas Child, John Bowman, and others, live. It is said this name originated from the following circumstance: The inhabitants that first settled this part of the town were in the habit of annually setting fire to the woods in the spring of the year, for the purpose of producing a young and tender growth of trees and plants for the subsistence of their cattle, not having pastures cleared up as we now have. Each one would put a bell upon the leader of his flock or herd or horse, for the purpose of finding them readily when wanted. Within my own recollection, the hills to the west of us were burned over every year for the purpose above stated; and the illumination occasioned thereby, for several successive nights, will probably never be effaced from my memory. This practice had almost destroyed the first growth of timber on the spot last mentioned, and the land was considered of very little value. Mr. Solomon Ager, who at that time was not considered a prophet nor the son of a prophet, had the hardihood to risk his all (as he had nothing to lose) by settling on this open tract of land. Some of his wiser neighbors attempting to ridicule him for selecting so barren a spot of land to get his living on, the old man replied, that "it would one day be the Flour of Warwick;" and ever after it has been called "Flour Hill."

The east part of the town towards Royalston, where Deacon Ebenezer Stearns, Mr. James Pierce, and others, live, probably from its being so rough and uneven, has sarcastically been called "Moose Plain." The north part of the town, where Messrs. Elisha Rich, David Ball, Amory Gale, and Justus Russell, Esqs., reside, is called "the Brook," originating from the stream of water that takes its rise near the middle of the town, and empties into the Ashuelot River, at Winchester, N.H., being called "Miry Brook." In the south part of the town, the land lying south of Morse's Pond was formerly called "Skunks Baron:" farther south, where Jonathan Shepardson lives, was called "Padanaram." The first name originated from the sterility of the soil, and the last from its being a plain, level spot. What is now the south-east corner of the town, where Messrs. Reuben Wheaton and Andrew Burnett live, was called "Peaked End," from the circumstance of there being no settled spot near them, they being considered the end of the settlement.

The two natural ponds obtained their names from the owners of the soil near them; viz., "Pomeroy's Pond," near the centre of the town, and Morse's Pond," a little farther to the south-west. The mountain near the middle of the town was called "Mount Grace," in consequence of a child of Mrs. Rowlandson's, whose name was "Grace," being buried somewhere near the foot of it. Mrs. Rowlandson, with her child, was taken captive by the Indians at Lancaster when that town was destroyed and sacked and burned. After the destruction of the town, the Indians proceeded on towards Canada with their captives; and this child died soon after they crossed "Miller's River," ten miles from Warwick; and Mrs. Rowlandson brought it in her arms, until she arrived near this mountain, where, compelled by fatigue, she reluctantly consigned it to the earth.*

* This was an early tradition, and then believed to be true; but it is not authenticated in Mrs. Rowlandson's history of her captivity.

The brook that takes its rise near the west side of this mountain is also called "Grace Brook," until it reaches "Morse's Pond;" and then it takes the name of "Morse's Brook." The brook that runs near William Hastings, James Ball, and through Caleb Mayo, Esq.'s, meadow, was formerly called "Black Brook:" farther south it takes the name of "Scott's Brook." The brook that runs near James Pierce's house is called "Tully Brook:" the name is derived from Tully River, this brook being the source of West Tully, as it is called; and East and West Tully unite, and empty into Miller's River, in Athol. The north-east part of Warwick, through which this brook passes, is called the "Kelton Corner." The name was derived from this circumstance: one Mr. Enoch Kelton, an early settler in the town, located himself on the spot where Peter Sandin now lives, and afterwards settled four or five of his sons around him, and lived in this patriarchal manner a considerable number of years.

Mr. Kelton was a land-surveyor: although his acquired attainments were rather limited, he was a good practical workman; the monuments that he erected bear ample testimony to that fact, even up to the present time.

His family afflictions, in one instance in particular, were uncommonly severe: his wife, for fifty long years before her death, was confined day and night to her bed.

The north-east lobe of Mount Grace has been called by a local name: one of the first settlers, Mr. Samuel Bennett, set down on home-lot No. 40. This lot lies on the side hill, east of the brook, sloping towards Mount Grace, below Abijah Fisher's house: the remains of the cellar, and a few apple-trees, are still witnesses of the exact spot. This Mr. Bennett said that one morning, as he stood in his door (which, by the way, faced this part of the mountain), he discovered a deer bounding along on the top of the Knob: he said he stepped back, and took down his gun, and fired, "and dropped the buck dead on the spot." His incredulous neighbors, amused with the idea of his killing a deer across the deep ravine, more than half a mile wide, that intervened between his house and the top of the hill in question, ever afterwards called it " Bennett's Knob."

This same Mr. Bennett and wife afterwards lived where Mr. Aaron Bass now lives; and Mrs. Bennett related a story, that, perhaps, is a little colored with the marvellous. The dwellings in those days were not exactly as they are at the present. Many of them were built with logs; and those that were framed, as well as those of logs, generally were, one end of them, principally occupied by the chimney, a huge mass of stones piled up as a back for the fireplace; and not unfrequently all that could be called a chimney was a hole in the top of the house to let out the smoke. Eight or ten feet was a fireplace of moderate size in those days; and some actually used a horse to haul in their back-logs. The house that our good old progenitors lived in was not out of the fashion. The stones of the chimney on either side, however, were not exactly fitted to the wooden part of the building, or they had settled away, so that there was a large crack at the side of the jambs, where they could see out.

Our heroine said she was sitting one evening, spinning on a foot-wheel, and, happening to look round to the side of the fire-place, she saw a bear looking in at the crack, — *she plainly saw his eyes glisten.* Bruin, after satisfying his curiosity, cleared for the woods.

I have a story to relate of the temerity of one of our first settlers. It was Mr. David Gale, father of the present David Gale, sen.: as he was chopping in the woods, near where the present David Gale now lives, with his son, a small lad, he discovered a monstrous animal in the woods; it was unlike any creature he had before seen. The wild beast, on being discovered, had immediate recourse to the top of a tree. Mr. Gale, as if unconscious of danger, left his little boy to watch the motions of the ferocious animal, with a charge to keep him on the tree: he went to his house, loaded his gun, returned to the place, and shot the animal, which proved to be nothing less than a full-grown catamount; and that was the only one that was ever killed in Warwick.

1738.

In the year 1738 a committee of the proprietors was appointed to find out the nearest route from Roxbury to this new tract of country; and a vote was passed, taxing each of the sixty proprietors, to raise the sum of six pounds apiece, as a bounty to encourage the first ten proprietors that shall settle, and comply with the conditions before mentioned by actually moving on, and building a house, &c.

1740.

In 1740 Deacon Davis was empowered to mark out a way through Pequeage (now Athol), and the said plantation, to Northfield. It is not now known exactly where this way was cleared out; but it is conjectured that it passed through the easterly and northerly part of the town, and went into Northfield, near where the old North-county road was afterwards laid.

The old records are silent, as to the proceedings of the proprietors of this new town, for about eight years; but it may be inferred from the prior proceedings, that the inducements to commence the settlement were not sufficient to allure the wealthy on the one hand, or to enable the poor on the other, to transport themselves and their families to this then unbroken forest, without roads, without means of conveyance, and without any thing to subsist on after their arrival.

1749.

In the year 1749 the bounty was increased to twenty pounds to each individual, as an inducement to settle, — ten pounds in advance, five pounds in one year, and five pounds more in two years after settlement.

1751.

In this year the proprietors voted to make up the bounty to thirty pounds (old tenor), or the value thereof in silver.

1753.

This year fifty pounds was voted to defray the expense of building a sawmill; and a spot was to be selected where it would accommodate the proprietors; and, at a meeting of the proprietors of "Gardner's Canada" (as this settlement was still called), it was voted, "to choose a committee to lay out and clear a road to Pequeage near the pond, south-eastwardly from the way proposed and marked to be laid out towards Royalston from Pequeage to the sawmill; and to come into the way marked out to go from Royalshire to Northfield." And they chose a committee to clear out said road. It was also voted that the committee for building the meeting-house be desired to proceed to accomplish that business: said house to be thirty-five feet long, and thirty feet wide, with nineteen-foot posts.

Said committee was also directed to appoint the spot where the meeting-house was to stand. The place selected by this committee to build said house on, and where the timber was collected and framed, was about forty or fifty rods south of Mr. Elijah Fisk's house; and it was subsequently moved and raised near where the present meeting-house now stands, for reasons hereafter to be related.

1754.

On the 7th of August this year, the committee for building made a report that Mr. Mason and Mr. Perry were willing to undertake said building, agreeable to the proposed dimensions, for twenty-six pounds, thirteen shillings, and fourpence, the proprietors to defray the expense of procuring the slitwork on the spot; and the said carpenters would make the said frame good, and in all respects workmanlike, and have it ready to raise by the first day of October next; or they would work by the day, and get it done by that time, at four shillings per day. It was voted by the proprietors that they should do it by the "great" for the sum proposed, the committee to defray the expense of the raising entertainment.

1755.

The committee for building the sawmill reported, on the 5th of March, that Mr. Ebenezer Locke, who had undertaken to build the mill in said township, informed them that some time in September last he had been at said township in order to finish said mill, and thought he should have finished the work in a little time; but some of the inhabitants of Northfield had advised him to leave the place if he had any regard for his life; for the Indians had done mischief in No. 4,[*] and in divers other places; and he had left it unfinished. The committee that was appointed to superintend the building of the meetinghouse also reported that the contractors had not performed their work; but had "only cut ten or twenty trees towards the frame." After considerable delay

---
[*] Now Charlestown, N.H.

and perplexity about the business, and several times lengthening the contract (or the time for performing the conditions of it), it was reported that the frame of the meeting-house was ready to be raised, but that a dispute had arisen as to the spot where it should stand.

1756.

On the 10th of March this year, it was voted to alter the spot where the meeting-house should stand, and fix it not exceeding one hundred and sixty rods to the north-east, where the road from Royalshire to Northfield was intersected by the road to the Pond. The meeting-house was raised by invitation of hands from Northfield and the adjacent settlements, on the twenty-eighth day of April, 1756.

In September this year, the proprietors having previously agreed to prosecute Ebenezer Locke on his bond for not erecting the sawmill, agreed to suspend the same on hearing his excuse. He stated that he had been retarded by reason of the war, and driven off, when at work on the premises, by the enemy's approaching near said township, and killing divers persons, and capturing others ; and afterwards, when he had been at the charge to get up to the work for the aforesaid purpose, the enemy made one other sally, and had killed Grout, Howe, and Garfield, and carried others into captivity. Sickness in his family, and burying his daughter, are among his excuses, and also having his men enlisted into his Majesty's service.

We can have but a very faint idea of the sufferings and hardships which our predecessors endured in their first attempt to settle this part of the country : the lurking, savage foe, at all times on the alert, ready to take them by surprise, to kill them, and to destroy the labor of their hands ; the wild beasts to haunt around their dwellings, and to tear and mangle their unguarded flocks ; the scanty means of procuring a subsistence, — hunger, poverty, and want staring them full in the face. It needed hearts of oak to successfully repel these varied buffetings of fortune ; and hearts of oak they verily had. How would many of the puny sons of indolence and ease at the present day have conducted, had they been placed under such trying circumstances ? They would have given up the ghost in a strange land.

1757.

On the sixth day of July, this year, eight pounds was voted to be allowed out of the treasury of the proprietors, "to fortify Mr. Samuel Scott's house, by making a good picketed fort encompassing the same, four rods square, for the safety of the inhabitants." This fort, which was the only one ever built in Warwick, was on land now owned by the Rev. John Goldsbury, and lies on the north side of the road that leads from Widow Jerusha Goldsbury's to William Hastings's ; and from this circumstance this piece of land has obtained the name of the "Old Fort," or the Fort Lot. The proprietors also voted four pounds to enclose the meeting-house.

1759.

Although four pounds was voted in 1757 to enclose the meeting-house, the frame was still standing at this date uncovered. But the sawmill, according to the old records, "was got a-going," so that the first sawmill that started in this town was set a-going seventy-two years ago. In May, this year, twenty-six pounds, thirteen shillings, and four pence was voted by the proprietors to build a gristmill; and a committee, consisting of Col. Joseph Williams, Mr. Joseph Majo, and Mr. Samuel Scott, was chosen, "to pitch on a suitable spot to build it on."

1760.

On May 21, 1760, it was voted "to raise the sum of eighteen pounds, lawful money, to defray the charge of some suitable orthodox minister's preaching upon probation within said township during the summer season:" and it is presumed that the Rev. Lemuel Hedge was the candidate that preached here that summer; for, on the 24th of September, they voted a hundred and forty-nine pounds, to be paid as follows: eighty pounds for Mr. Hedge's settlement, and sixty pounds for his first year's salary, and nine pounds for defraying the expense of his ordination.

Thus you see that the institutions of religion and morality, were not neglected by our predecessors. Although poor, and hard pressed in their temporal affairs, they cheerfully devoted a part of it for the promotion of Christianity; for they further voted that they would agree to pay sixty pounds a year for five years to come, until some other suitable provision for Mr. Hedge's support should be made, provided he settled with them. A committee was chosen, consisting of Capt. David Ayres, Moses Evans, Israel Olmstead, Ebenezer Prescott, and Amzi Doolittle, "to treat with Mr. Hedge respecting his settlement here." At the same meeting they chose the same committee, with the addition of Mr. Joshua Bailey, to lay out a tract of land forty rods square around the meeting-house in said township, for a burying-place, training-field, and other public uses. This tract is what we now call the *common*, and contains ten acres of land: the name doubtless originated from its being laid out of what was then called common land; viz., lands not surveyed and divided among the sixty original proprietors. Thus, without detriment to themselves, or any sacrifice of property to be by them felt at the time, they secured to the public a small patrimony, to be enjoyed by us and all succeeding generations that may come after us. And further still, for the accommodation of their minister, provided he settled with them, they voted that he might have the liberty to lay out a hundred acres of land near the meeting-house, in one piece, out of any of the common lands, to be laid in regular form, in lieu of the hundred acres in the after-division (or second division) of land, that would fall to the minister's right. Subsequently the hundred acres where Mr. Stephen Reed now lives were laid out to Mr. Hedge. Messrs. James Goldsbury, Asa Wheeler, Rev. Preserved Smith (our present pastor), William Cobb, Esq., Col. Lemuel Wheelock, and Samuel P. Damon, are all of them located on this hundred-acre lot, although it runs southerly to Pomeroy's Pond. The committee chosen to *treat* with Mr. Hedge respecting his settlement here in the gospel ministry no doubt performed their duty; for we find by the old records Mr. Hedge's answer to their call, as follows: —

To the Committee of the Proprietors of Roxbury Canada (so called) chosen to treat with me respecting my settling in said township.

GENTLEMEN, — Whereas the proprietors of Roxbury Canada (so called), at their meeting on the 24th of September, 1760, voted certain sums of money for a settlement and salary, and likewise granted me liberty of laying out one hundred acres of land near the meeting-house in said place (as per their vote may appear), in case I would settle there in the work of the gospel ministry, and the inhabitants of said township having by subscription made an addition to my settlement, and engage to find me annually thirty-five cords of wood, I have taken the matter into serious consideraton, and hereby inform you that I accept of this invitation to settle in this place.

LEMUEL HEDGE.

1761.

On Nov. 12, of this year, the proprietors were for the first time notified to meet in the meeting-house, in said township, to transact their business (having always met in Roxbury before this time). There were at that time thirty-seven settlers or families located on the first division of lots. Mr. Joseph Perry lived where Mr. Joseph Willson now lives; George Robbins where Alexander Blake, Ebenezer Davis where the widow Drake, Edward Allen where Capt. John Stearns, Thomas Rich where Medad Pomeroy, Barnabas Russell where James Ball, Moses Leonard where Eliphaz Gould, and David Ayres and David Ayres, jun., where Miss Fanny Simonds now lives.

About this time a gristmill was built on Black Brook, where the first sawmill also stood: the land is now owned by Capt. James Goldsbury; and said mills stood a little west of William Hastings's dwelling-house, south of the road that leads to Samuel Goldsbury's from said Hastings's. In this early stage of the settlement, and until the gristmill was built, the hardy and industrious *"forlorn hope"* of Warwick suffered severely for the want of accommodations which we now enjoy: they were obliged to go a great distance out of the settlement to get their grain ground; and perhaps many times that was not the worst part of it, for many of them were poor, and had but little grain to grind. It was frequently the case that they had to go miles on foot to Northfield, or Athol, or farther still, to buy a peck of corn and get it ground, and then to bring it home on their backs. Nor was this all; for there were instances of their going to Northfield to buy hay, and bringing it home in the same way, to save their cattle alive. It was thought in those days, that, if their hay lasted until the 1st of March, they could get their cattle through the winter.

Seventy-two pounds was voted, this year, to finish the meeting-house; and it was agreed to build a pew on one side or the other of the pulpit, for Mr. Hedge, he being permitted to choose the side.

To show how valuable the land was in this town at this time, it appears that lot No. 7, and all the after-rights in said town, was sold at auction for £4. 5s. 8d., which was only about four cents and three mills per acre; but such sales were of rare occurrence, and perhaps were never known after.

Messrs. Elisha Rich, George Robbins, James Ball, and Asa Robbins were chosen a committee to lay out the common lands in said township into two divisions, the first to contain seventy-five acre lots, and the other to be left discretionary with the committee; and they accordingly laid out the last into sixty-six acre lots. These two divisions constitute what we call the third and fourth divisions of lands in this town. The third-division lots contain seventy-five acres, and the fourth sixty-six acres, each.

1762.

On the twenty-seventh day of December, 1762, it was voted that the proprietors join with the inhabitants of the plantation, to petition the General Court to be incorporated into a town. Col. Joseph Williams and Capt. Caleb Dana were chosen a committee to join with said inhabitants in the petition.

1763.

On the seventeenth day of February, 1763, this

tract of country was incorporated by the General Court as a town, by the name of *Warwick*.

How the name originated is not now known; but probably from Warwick in England, or from the famous " Guy, Earl of Warwick."

We have now arrived at the time, you will probably say, that I ought to have commenced my remarks, or where I might have begun with propriety the history of the town. From this period down to the present time we have a tolerably regular and legible record of most of the public proceedings of the town. I shall not follow the records, by noting every little local transaction that has happened in our public or private affairs, but shall select and abridge a few of the most interesting events, for our mutual instruction, and for the benefit of posterity.

When we wish to make an inquiry about any particular place or thing, the first question that suggests itself to our mind is, where, when, or how, did it happen or begin? How, when, and where the municipal proceedings of Warwick originated, shall be our first subject of inquiry.

In the third year of his Majesty's reign, Seth Field, Esq., of Northfield, by order of the General Court, issued a warrant to James Ball of Warwick, to notify the inhabitants of said town to attend the first town-meeting. Said meeting was directed to be warned by posting up a notification in some public place in said township, fourteen days before the time of holding the same. This meeting was convened the ninth day of May, A.D. 1763, at nine o'clock in the morning. Seth Field, Esq., acted as moderator; James Ball was chosen clerk; Moses Evans, Jeduthan Morse, and James Ball, selectmen and assessors; Amzi Doolittle, treasurer; Samuel Ball, constable; James Ball, collector; Silas Town and Joshua Bailey, wardens; Charles Wood and Joseph ———, tything-men; Israel Olmsted and Moses Leonard, fence-viewers; Moses Leonard, Joseph Lawrence, and Joseph Goodell, hog-reeves; David Barrett, pound-keeper: Ebenezer Davis, field-driver; Amos Marsh and Moses Leonard, deer-reeves; Moses Evans, culler of staves, shingles, and clapboards; James Ball, scaler of weights and measures; Moses Leonard, scaler of leather. It was voted that hogs may go at large on the common.

On the 16th of June following, the second town-meeting was held; and they voted to Esq. Paine twenty shillings for services at the General Court in getting the town incorporated; and Mr. James Ball was to pay him the money, and return the town's thanks. Voted twenty pounds for highways, and started the work at four shillings per day for a man, and two shillings for a yoke of oxen, and one shilling for a cart or plough. They also voted that the selectmen should draw a petition to the General Court, that the westerly part of the county of Worcester, and the easterly part of the county of Hampshire, may be set off, and erected into a distinct and separate county.

At this meeting, the committee chosen for the purpose of treating with Mr. Hedge respecting his future support was directed to condense the proposals formerly made into the form of an agreement, and to have it recorded on the town-book.

Which agreement was as follows: viz., "That the town will pay to the Rev. Mr. Hedge a salary of sixty pounds until such time as there shall be eighty settled families in said town ; and the salary to rise as the families increase, allowing thirteen shillings and fourpence to each family: so that when there should be ninety settled families the salary would amount to sixty-six pounds, thirteen shillings, and fourpence ; and after that, allowing four shillings and fivepence to a family, when they had increased to one hundred and fifty families, his salary should be eighty pounds, to be paid in lawful silver money, at six shillings and eightpence per ounce ; and, annually, thirty cords of wood, cut eight feet long, delivered at his door." Mr. Hedge acknowledged these proposals handsome and generous, and put his signature to them July 4, 1763. Nov. 28, the same year, James Ball, Israel Olmsted, and Silas Town were chosen a committee to finish the meeting-house. June 15, this year, the selectmen laid out the first town-road (on record). They began at or near the line of Richmond, N.H., near where Mr. Caleb Weeks now lives, and laid said road southerly, by Thomas Mallard's, Dea. Samuel Ball's, and Capt. Josiah Proctor's, to Lot No. 51, in the second division, to Samuel Ball's house ; said road to be three rods wide ; and another road, two rods wide, by Moses Leonard's house (now Eliphaz Gould's) ; viz., within one rod of it, to the county-road.

1764.

May 30, of this year, there is a charge on the

town-book of fifteen shillings, for James Ball, Mr. Evans, and Mr. Nourse taking the invoice, and Mr. Morse making the highway-tax. We should think that this charge was not extravagant. This year the town accepted of a road, laid from the common, southerly by Elijah Fisk's, and where Stephen Johnson lately lived, to Morse's Pond and Locke's Mills, where Mr. Francis Leonard's sawmill now is: said road to be three rods wide. Also a road beginning at the north-west corner of Benjamin Conant's house, which intersected the last-mentioned road near where Mr. Elijah Fisk now lives: this road was laid all the way on the top of the hill, west of the Widow Hannah Rich and Isaiah Bang's houses. Traces of this road are now visible in many places, almost directly on the ridge, south of Mr. Fisk's. Also another road, commencing where Mr. Jonas Leonard now lives, by Mr. Asa Ware's, to intersect the one that leads to Morse's Pond, at the Stephen Johnson place. No width si given to this road.

1765.

This year forty pounds was voted to be raised to repair highways; and it was also voted that the selectmen should take care of Elizabeth Rumble and her children, and receive them as *town's poor* (these are the first paupers mentioned); and in November this year, the town granted ten pounds, eight shillings, to be proportioned on the inhabitants according to their invoice, to defray the expense of keeping said paupers one year; and that the inhabitants shall all have to keep said woman and her children their proportions of said rate.

1766.

Voted to choose five selectmen this year; and chose Benjamin Conant, James Ball, Jeduthan Morse, Amos Marsh, and Amzi Doolittle; and chose Jeduthan Morse, Ebenezer Curtis, and Amos Marsh, assessors; raised forty pounds to support the highways, and voted two shillings to Asa ———, for keeping Sarah Rumble three weeks. The first three selectmen this year laid out a burying-ground, as follows: viz., " Beginning at the north-west corner of the meeting-house common, and extending east, on the north line, to a small hemlock-tree, marked for the north-east corner; thence south, seven degrees east, to a black-oak-tree; then due south, twelve rods, to a stake and stones; thence west, to the west line of the common; thence north, to the first-mentioned corner."

1768.

At a town-meeting convened at the meeting-house, March 7, the town voted ten pounds to support a school some part of the year. It was then proposed to the town, whether they would have a moving school? and it was voted in the affirmative: also voted to have a school kept December, January, and February, by a master; and the remainder of the ten pounds to pay a mistress to keep school in the summer season; and voted that the selectmen employ a master and mistress, and appoint the school wards, or places, where the schools shall be kept.

This is the first account that we have of a school being kept at the expense of the town, and, we presume, the first attempt to district the town. In June following, a town-meeting was called, to see if the town would sell a school-lot, and to give the selectmen instructions concerning a woman's school: and they voted that Mrs. Hannah Rawson be employed to keep school; and they further voted, that, if the major part of the quarter where she lived objected against her keeping, the selectmen should dismiss her; or, if the selectmen found any material objection against her, they should dismiss her; and she is to have four shillings and six pence per week for the time she keeps, her father finding her board.

1769.

In 1769, ten pounds was raised for schooling, and the selectmen clothed with the same authority as last year, — hiring, districting, &c.

1770 AND '71.

In 1771, the town voted twelve pounds for schooling, and sixty pounds to be worked out on the roads.

In the year 1770, the proprietors chose a committee, consisting of James Ball, Nathan Goddard, and Samuel Williams, to lay out the fifth and last division of lands in Warwick. They employed a surveyor by the name of Job Gilbert, and laid out sixty-two lots, containing a little over fourteen acres each. These lots were laid out of the several pieces of common land remaining in various forms in different parts of the town. Where they began, they laid off as many lots as the piece would make, and the fraction that remained would be numbered, and acres enough taken off the next piece (of the same number) to make out the fourteen acres. They thus proceeded until they had surveyed off all the fragments of land in the town. This accounts for the parts of the fourteen-acre lots being so scattered; for instance, N. G. Stevens, jun., owns part of a lot adjoining Capt. William Burnett's farm, containing five or six acres; and the remainder of the lot lies south of Israel Fisher's land. William Perry owns part of a lot south of his house, and the other part is not far from William Hastings's. There is a record of a vote of the old proprietors in 1769, in these words: —

"Provided always, that it is the true intent and meaning of this proprietary, that all the several slips that were reserved for roads, between any or all of the first and second division of lands in said township, be and remain for the use of the inhabitants of said town from time to time, and at all times forever hereafter, for roads or highways; and may be exchanged by said inhabitants, for other lands for roads more to the town's advantage."

* This may be considered as a good title, or right and privilege to the public, that has been little regarded, and perhaps not generally known. After this last division was laid out, there remained one hundred and

six acres of land to the original proprietors. It was voted to raise a tax of two dollars on each share, and give the town the one hundred and six acres of land, for them to finish off the meeting-house. The town declined the accepting of the offer of the land, as Francis Nourse and Josiah Rawson had laid claim to and entered upon said land.*

Nothing of particular importance is found on the town records for several years; but we are now approaching a crisis full of interest and big with events; and future generations will look back with astonishment, reverence, and awe at the mighty deeds and the powerful exertions of the generations that have immediately preceded us. To this generation, under the blessing of God, we are indebted for all the civil privileges we now enjoy. And not only we, but the whole human race, may commemorate this era as the first dawning of the light of liberty.

Here, in this new world, in this then thinly-populated country, just emerging into political life, were nursed and cherished the first pure principles of civil and religious freedom. Who of us can restrain our feelings? Who can stifle the flame of gratitude that bursts involuntarily from the sacred depositories of our hearts? Who that has the spirit and mind of a freeman can undervalue these privileges, and not reciprocate and rejoice with every true defender of his country, every worshipper of his God?

At the breaking out of the Revolutionary War, the inhabitants of this town were not a whit behind their

* This was the last vote on record of the doings of the old proprietors.

neighbors in principle or practice: the same spirit of liberty that echoed throughout New England responded from our fathers and our brethren. A mighty impulse pervaded the whole population. "*Liberty or death*" was their motto. The proud spirit of our fathers bade defiance to British thunder; the bright and dazzling equipments of regular and well-disciplined troops could not intimidate the hardy yeomanry of our country. I will here relate a story, strictly characteristic of our countrymen: I had it from the mouth of an eye-witness,* who was a brother to one of Gen. Washington's life-guards. It was at the taking of Cornwallis. The regiment that this man belonged to had, previous to that event, suffered unnumbered privations, were continually on the alert, and their clothing was literally rags: he said nearly one-half of the regiment were barefoot; but their hearts were as true as the needle to the pole. The supplies which had been long expected from the government had not arrived; but, by perseverance and valor, the day of their deliverance was at hand. At this critical period, when the fate of our country was suspended by a thread, the summons from the American camp struck terror and dismay into the heart of the haughty British commander. He made a conditional surrender, and the time was set when his troops should march out of the post, and stack their arms. Our allies, the French, were drawn up in a long line on one side, and the Americans on the other; and the British troops, the prisoners, were to march out between these lines, with

---

* Mr. James Davenport of Dorchester, Mass.

4*

trailed arms, unloaded, and deposit them on the spot assigned. Our brave Yankees literally toed the line, for their feet were many of them bare; while the proud British soldiers were dressed, as the saying is, "neat as a new pin," — every man had his hair powdered, and every one was a prince to look to. My informant said that language was too feeble to describe the indignation and resentment of the British soldiers, plainly depicted in their countenances, to think that they had surrendered to such a dirty, ragged, weatherbeaten set of human beings: they gnashed their teeth, and shook their heads, and muttered out oaths and execrations too horrid to rehearse. All the while our victorious countrymen stood firm and unmoved, — guns loaded, swords drawn, hearts of steel: a glow of manly enthusiasm and joy beamed from every countenance; while the rude winds of heaven sported with their tattered garments. This was truly American; this was truly the character of our fathers: though poor and destitute, they were powerful, energetic, and brave, and never bowed the knee to, nor owned a superior in, any human being. This regiment that I have mentioned was presented, by the great and good Lafayette, with shoes and stockings, and every one of the sergeants with a cutlass, out of his own private purse, as a reward for their integrity, obedience, and devotedness to the cause of liberty. He never deserted them by day or by night; and when the soldiers were obliged to encamp on the ground, in the open field, he would refuse, when solicited to accept of better fare, and lie down on the ground by the side of his horse, and in company with his men. How strange, how astonishing, that a young and rich nobleman, born with an ample fortune, should leave the land of his birth, the friends of his youth, the gay and fascinating pleasures so alluring to the young, and repair to a foreign land, to espouse their cause, to fight their battles, to associate with and become attached to our rude and rustic sires! But such was the case; and what could be the cause? what reason can we assign for it? It was the principles of the man, the congenial feelings, the attachment, the indissoluble attachment of kindred souls,— an attachment which adversity cannot weaken nor death destroy.

1774.

A meeting was called " in His Majesty's name " (but not in obedience to His Majesty) on the thirtieth day of August, 1774, to take into consideration several papers sent to the town of Warwick from the town of Boston, and from committees of correspondence, to see if the town will enact any thing respecting these papers, or any thing else relating to the public difficulties that this Province labors under at this day; and also to see if the town will make a grant of the sum desired to defray the charges of the committee of Congress.

Now listen: This meeting was called, or notified, on the 30th of August. See the promptitude, see the ardency of their feelings: unable to wait seven days, as the law required, they are summoned to meet on the fifth day of September, at two o'clock, P.M. Not a voice is raised to dispute the legality of the meeting, but a simultaneous response of "Forward! forward! Our rights are invaded, our liberties are in jeopardy." But let us pause, and hear their simple but energetic language :—

"Voted and chose Mr. Ezra Conant moderator. Voted the sum of eight shillings, being this town's proportion of the sum agreed on by the Honorable Council and House of Representatives in their session to pay a committee of Congress. Voted to get two barrels of powder, and lead and flints, answerable for a town stock ; and that the selectmen be a committee to procure the same. Voted to adhere strictly to our chartered rights and privileges, and to defend them to the utmost of our capacity; and that we will be in readiness, that, if our brethren in Boston or elsewhere should be distressed by the troops sent here to force a compliance to the unconstitutional and oppressive acts of the British Parliament, and will give us notice, that we will repair to their relief forthwith. Voted to choose a captain, lieutenant, and ensign, and that they enlist fifty men in this town to be at a minute's warning to go, if called for, to the relief of our brethren in any part of the Province.

"Voted and chose Samuel Williams captain ; James Ball lieutenant ; and Amzi Doolittle ensign. Voted that the expenses of said company (if called to go) shall be paid by the town, an account therefor being exhibited to the town by officers thereof."

Signed by EZRA CONANT, *Moderator.*

Here you may see the unanimity of kindred souls ; here is a fair sample of our fathers' characters in those gloomy and perilous times, volunteering their property, and all that was dear to them as men, or valuable to them as citizens, — yes, and their lives too, — on the sacred altar of their country's rights. But my story is not yet half told; for, on the 17th of September, "Joseph Mayo, constable of said town, was directed forthwith to notify the inhabitants thereof to assemble on the 19th instant at three o'clock in the afternoon, to see if the town will vote to choose delegates to represent them in a county congress, to be convened at Northampton on the 22d instant, at nine o'clock in the morning; also to see if the town will act any thing respecting our public affairs, and choose such committee or committees, and give them instructions as they shall think proper at said meeting." Here again the constable was directed on Saturday to summon the people to meet on Monday, to act on matters of the first importance. Where was the law? The impulse of the moment was their law, their conscience their law-giver, and their God their judge. But they assembled, every man to his post, and chose Capt. Samuel Williams moderator. It was proposed to the town to send delegates to the congress at Northampton on the 22d, and immediately voted in the affirmative. Voted and chose Capt. Samuel Williams and Mr. Josiah Pomeroy delegates. Also voted that an attested copy of the proceedings of this meeting be given to the delegates by the town clerk; then adjourned the meeting to the 26th instant, at four o'clock, P.M.

Met again at the time specified at the adjournment, instructed and animated by their delegates, who had returned from Northampton. They voted to send Capt. Samuel Williams to represent them in a Provincial Congress, to be holden at Concord, on the second Tuesday of October following.

A town meeting was convened Nov. 7, to pass upon and pay the costs of the delegation to Northampton and Concord; also to see if the town will choose their militia officers, or divide the town into two companies; viz., an alarm-list company, and a training company, of militia. It may be necessary to state, for information, that the above company just mentioned consisted of all the exempts from the militia companies by reason of age. The law at that day compelled the militiamen to train until they were forty-five years of age; and the alarm-list consisted of all able-bodied men between forty-five and sixty years of age. The old men between forty-five and sixty years were obliged to keep themselves constantly armed and equipped, and to meet for inspection and training only once a year, but were obliged to turn out at the call of the authority of the State.

At this meeting, the town voted to pay Samuel Williams his account for attending the county congress at Northampton, as follows: viz., For four days' time, eight shillings; journey of his horse, five shillings; and travelling expenses, five shillings: amounting to eighteen shillings. Also voted to pay Mr. Josiah Pomeroy the same sum. They also voted to pay Capt. Samuel Williams for attending the Provincial Congress at Concord, eighteen days, at two shillings per day, and twelve shillings for the journey of his horse, and his expenses three shillings per day.

These charges speak volumes in favor of the disinterestedness of the men who served the public in those days. The town then proceeded to choose a captain of the militia, and chose Samuel Williams; Peter Proctor lieutenant; and Reuben Petty ensign; and Amos Marsh clerk. At an adjournment of this meeting, the town voted to choose two lieutenants for said company, and chose the aforesaid Peter Proctor first lieutenant, and Reuben Petty the second, and Thomas Rich ensign; and voted that the company should choose their under-officers. You may possibly think that I have been too lavish of my encomiums, — that I have said too much in commendation of the actors on the stage at the time we have been considering. But I think that too much cannot be said. I think their conduct to be above all praise; but I do not deny that they were men, and men, too, of like passions and propensities with ourselves, subject to error, and frequently erring. But where they acted bravely and disinterestedly, they ought to have the praise of it. Infirmities they all probably had, — and infirmities we all have at the present day; let us pattern after their virtues, and avoid their imperfections.

In the autumn of 1774 the first appearance of discord on religious matters in this town appears on record. One article in the warrant was as follows: viz., "To see if the town will take into consideration the certificates of the differing societies of those persons that call themselves Baptists in this town; and pass any votes respecting their being taxed to the minister, any or all of them."

They voted to Aaron Whitney eight pounds for the two kegs of powder; three pounds and fourpence for two hundred weight of lead and three hundred flints; and transport of the articles, one pound and nine shillings; making twelve pounds, nine shillings, and fourpence. And they also voted that twenty-seven persons, expressed by name on the records, should not be rated to the minister.

This year the town granted eighty pounds for repair of highways, forty pounds of it to be worked on the county road: three-fourths of the money to be worked out before the middle of July, the other fourth before the 1st of October; and it was also voted that the wages on the highway should be three shillings for a man, two shillings for a yoke of oxen, and one shilling for a cart or plough per day. Twenty-four pounds (including the interest) was voted for schooling.

It was omitted in its proper place to mention the first division of this town into school-districts. June 3, 1773, the town voted to choose a committee of five, to divide the whole town into school-districts; said division, when made, to be binding on the town, entry thereof being made on the town-book by order of the selectmen. Said committee consisted of Messrs. Jonathan Woodard, Ezra Conant, James Ball, Dr. Medad Pomeroy, and Amos Marsh.

1775.

Jan. 3 of this year, a meeting was convened to see if the town would choose a man to send to

Cambridge, to the Provincial Congress in February next; and to see if the town will accept the proposals agreed upon by the selectmen and a committee chosen by the Baptist society, to leave our lawsuit that the Baptists commenced against James Ball, Medad Pomeroy, and Ezra Conant, at the last May sessions.

Voted and chose Samuel Williams to represent the town at Cambridge. Voted to pass over the last article. March 6, 1775, it was voted to choose five selectmen; and Amos Marsh, Samuel Williams, Josiah Pomeroy, Thomas Rich, and David Cobb were chosen; Amos Marsh town clerk. Seventy pounds was voted for highways. The twenty-ninth article acted on at this meeting. It was moved and voted that they choose a committee of inspection consisting of five men; and they chose Reuben Petty chairman, Seth Peck, Josiah Pomeroy, Thomas Rich, and Amos Marsh, said committee.

May 18, it was voted to reconsider the vote passed at the last annual meeting respecting the grant of money for the highways; and they voted instead, thirty-five pounds, — twenty pounds to be worked on the county road. They also voted to send a man to the Provincial Congress, and chose Samuel Williams. The July following, Col. Samuel Williams was again chosen a delegate to a court or congress to be convened in the meeting-house in Watertown; and the town chose three men a committee to give him his instructions; viz., Amos Marsh, Thomas Rich, and Seth Peck.

Also voted, the inhabitants do concur with the resolve and recommend of the committees of correspondence of Northfield, Athol, and Warwick, to disarm and confine the Rev. Mr. Hedge to the town of Warwick, unless he has a permit from the committee of correspondence of said town. Voted to choose eleven men as a committee to come into some plan to settle the difficulties between this people and Mr. Hedge; viz., Amos Marsh, Ezra Conant, Samuel Williams, Peter Proctor, Moses Leonard, Jonathan Woodard, Jeduthan Morse, Abraham Barnes, Samuel Sherman, Benjamin Conant; and the record states that the eleventh man was not chosen, by reason of a miscount. Meeting adjourned to July 17.

The adjourned meeting having assembled, the committee on Mr. Hedge's matters made a report, as follows: viz., Mr. Hedge proposes that he will, upon the town's rescinding the vote to disarm and confine him to said town, pledge his honor that he will not influence or prejudice the minds of the people against the common cause which the country is engaged in, and will then join with the town in three proposals: viz., First, to leave it to the General Assembly of the Province; second, to a mutual council; third, to any set of judicious men the town and he could agree upon.

On the report being made, a motion was made to rescind the vote; but it passed in the negative, as the records say, by a vast majority. The town then voted and chose Seth Peck, Jeduthan Morse, Daniel Gale, and Savill Metcalf, in addition to the committee of correspondence.

In September, a meeting was called to see if the selectmen should be authorized to purchase a quantity of salt for the use of the inhabitants, and have instructions for retailing the same. Also to see if the town will dismiss Mr. Hedge from his ministerial office; and to rescind the vote passed at the annual meeting, granting him his salary according to contract. These articles were all passed over; and seventy-two yeas for dismissing Mr. Hedge entered their protest against the vote. Voted to accept Col. Samuel Williams's account for attending the Congress, — two pounds ten shillings.

1776.

In March, 1776, the town chose five selectmen (the first three to be assessors), and also chose seven men a committee of correspondence, inspection, and safety; viz., Josiah Pomeroy, Josiah Rawson, Daniel Gale, Thomas Rich, Reuben Petty, Elijah Whitney, and Joseph Goodell. Voted forty pounds for repairing roads, and twenty-four pounds for schooling.

On the 24th of May, a meeting was convened for choosing a delegate or representative to meet on the 29th of May, at Watertown, in the General Assembly of the Province. This was the first town-meeting called in the name of the government and people of the Massachusetts Bay, all previous meetings having been called in the name of *His Majesty;* and at this meeting the first legal representative was chosen to represent the town: those that had been previously chosen were in defiance of a constituted authority. Lieut. Thomas Rich was chosen; and it was voted to choose a committee of three men to give instructions to said representative. Chose Amos Marsh, Josiah Rawson, and Reuben Petty. Then it was voted to adjourn the meeting half an hour, for said committee to draw instructions, and report to the town.

The meeting was opened agreeably to adjournment, and the committee read their instructions to the town; also a number of resolves of the committee of the county of Suffolk. The town then voted to accept said instructions, and also the sixth clause in the Suffolk resolves. Also voted that the said instructions, and the sixth clause of the Suffolk resolves, " goes on the town book." By this vote, those first instructions are preserved; and it will not injure us, if it does not profit us, to hear the sentiments they contain. They are as follows; viz. : —

"Whereas you, Lieut. Thomas Rich, are chosen to represent the town of Warwick in a General Assembly of the Colony of the Massachusetts Bay, we your constituents do give you the following instructions : —

" 1st, That you represent us, as true and loyal subjects to the power now in the hands of the people of America, and that you do your endeavour that no act or acts be passed encroaching on the liberties or in any measure invading the rights of the People.

" 2dly, That you grant all supplies necessary for the safety of America under her distressing circumstances; and that you are not extravagant in your grants to those that may be employed in the service of the Colony; at the same time trusting that every true friend to his country will be willing to serve in any place where he may be wanted, for a reasonable reward.

"3dly, That you tolerate all persuasions on account of their religious sentiments, without giving one the advantage of the other, either in their persons or their properties.

"4thly, That all such laws as in any degree infringe on the liberties of the people be made void. In particular, that of a person having twenty pounds ratable estate, to qualify him to vote in town affairs, by reason of which so great a majority as two-thirds of the freeholders of this town are prohibited voting in town affairs, although they pay the major part of the taxes hereby raised, which is frequently the case in new-settled towns. There are other things that are a burden, such as these : going sixty miles for license to keep tavern, and recording Deeds, all which may be done in every town, or in sundry places in the County, greatly to the advantage of the towns lying in the outside of the Counties.

"5thly, As also, paying the Representatives by their own towns, which might be more equitably done by the Province : a great hardship that a town of forty families should pay as much for the legislative power as one that has three hundred families in it ; and as we are poor, and hard drove to pay our taxes, every thing that is a burden that can be taken off or eased ought to be done.

"6thly, That all deceased wills be proved and recorded, and estates settled, in each town where the deceased last lived, by the Selectmen and Town Clerk in the same town ; and that each town have liberty, at each annual March meeting, to choose a Committee or Town Council to prove Wills and settle Estates, and a Register to record Wills and Settlements of Estates. Said Selectmen or Committee, and the Town Clerk or Register's fees, to be each year agreed upon by the same town."

Here in these instructions you see the jealousy of

our fathers, their republican principles, their love of liberty and equality, and above all, though miserably poor, their determination to support the cause of their country.

At a meeting of the inhabitants of the town of Warwick, July 4, 1776 (this meeting was called in compliance with a resolve of the General Court to express their sentiments on declaring Independence of the Kingdom of Great Britain), a motion was made and seconded, that the town *will* express their sentiments by declaring for independence by yeas and nays; and all that are not present at this meeting have the opportunity of giving their names to the town clerk within six days from said meeting, by personally appearing before said clerk; and voted, that the town clerk give off the sentiments relative to independence to Lieut. Thomas Rich, the representative for said town. Thirty-eight names voted *yea ;* and forty-four more came in within six days and voted for Independence : making a total of eighty-two *yeas*, and not one in the negative.

A handbill was circulated through the State, and a meeting called, to get the opinion of the inhabitants respecting a constitution and form of government in the several towns. This meeting was in October, 1776 ; and it was voted in this town, that the present House of Representatives, with the Council, should not enact and agree on a constitution or form of government, but that they should report one, and send it out to the towns, for their inspection and perusal ; and they chose a committee to frame instructions for the representative of the town. Chose Amos Marsh, Josiah

Rawson, and Peter Fish. Said instructions were as follows; viz.: —

To Mr. Thomas Rich.

Sir, — Having by a late vote empowered and directed you to join the other members of the General Assembly in forming a plan of Government for this State, and being fully sensible that it is a matter of the greatest importance, both to the present and future generations, that such a plan be adopted as shall be most free from the *seeds of tyranny*, and have the greatest tendency to preserve the rights and liberties of the people, and the most likely to preserve peace and good order in the State, we therefore beg leave to lay before you the following short hints respecting a form of government, which we apprehend, if adopted, will have a tendency to answer the purposes above mentioned.

1st, That there be but one branch in the legislative authority of this State; viz., the representatives from the several towns, with a president or speaker at the head.

2dly, That an equal representation may be made, and the balance of power properly preserved, let each incorporated town send one member, and the larger towns not more than four or five, and the other towns in equal proportion.

3dly, That in making choice of the representative, every free male inhabitant, twenty-one years of age, to have the privilege of voting.

4thly, That in case sufficient evidence appears to a town that their representative or members are guilty of acting contrary to the rights and liberties of the people, then to have the privilege, at any time in the year, to recall him or them, and choose anew.

5thly, That not less than eighty members make a house.

1777.

On Feb. 14, 1777, there is an account allowed by the town, in the following form : —

The town of Warwick to the Selectmen, Dr.

For numbering the people, in the year 1776, agreeably to a resolve of Congress, and act of the Court of the State of Massachusetts Bay. One day and an half each, at four shillings per day: the whole £1. 10s. 0d.

We notice this record, because it coincides with our opinion, that it is much the best way of numbering the people, — the cheapest and the most accurate. March 31, 1777, chose five Selectmen, and seven men as a Committee of Correspondence and Inspection and Safety. Forty pounds was raised for highways, half of it to be worked on the county roads; and twenty-four pounds, with the interest money, for schooling.

Thomas Rich was chosen Representative.

In August the town met, and voted to pay Josiah Cobb and Asahel Newton twelve pounds twelve shillings, to defray the expense of getting the salt from Boston, apportioned to them by the General Court.

About this time the depreciation in the paper money caused many embarrassments; and a meeting was called to take into consideration a late act of the General Court, in calling in the State's money, and granting treasury notes upon interest. And it was voted, that if no other method could be adopted than to call in the State's money and put it upon interest, that we would have said money called in and burned, rather than to run our risk in paying interest for it at a day when money cannot be had so easy as at the present day. Also voted, that the town will make choice of Caleb Strong for their County Register.

1778.

March 30, 1778, voted to choose five selectmen; and chose Amos Marsh, Lieut. Joseph Mayo, Lieut. Thomas Rich, Lieut. Josiah Pomeroy, and Caleb Mayo; and it was voted that the second, third, and fourth selectmen be assessors. Four hundred pounds was voted to repair the highways, half of it to be laid out on the County roads. Voted to allow twenty shillings a day for a man, ten shillings for a yoke of oxen, and six shillings for a cart or plough.*

Voted to set off Richard Wastcoat and the inhabitants about him, as a school ward.

May 21, 1778, a constitution or form of government was laid before the people in the several towns in this commonwealth. The vote in Warwick was three for adopting said constitution, and twenty-four against it.

Sept. 18, a meeting was held to see if the town will pay a bounty on wolves; and also to see if the town will provide preaching in said town, upon the plan of a free contribution; also to choose a committee to procure the same, upon the plan above mentioned; and also to see what measures the town will take to support the widow Sarah Crossman.

* This shows that the money was depreciated, by allowing such a price for labor.

Voted at the foregoing meeting to pay a bounty of twenty pounds per head on wolves; and proposed joining with Northfield, Winchester, Royalston, and Athol;. and voted that the selectmen be a committee to send to said towns.

Voted to pass over the article for procuring preaching.

Voted that Josiah Rawson and Samuel Mellen be a committee to provide for the widow Sarah Crossman the necessaries of life; and chose Dea. James Ball to look into the affair relative to the widow Crossman being an inhabitant of said town.

The crisis is passed and gone, which was so full of interest and instruction. The "breaking out" (as it has many times been expressed) of the "Revolutionary war," and the many heroic displays of the generation which has immediately preceded us, have in some measure eclipsed the many meritorious acts of the subsequent times. The most important, the *long to be remembered transaction*, that of declaring ourselves a *free and independent people or nation*, had passed by. But much remained yet to be done. The patience, the unexampled patience and fortitude, of our fathers and brothers, was severely tested.

In the midst of a noble struggle for *liberty* and the rights of man, they steadily and firmly stemmed the unequal contest,—a contest unexampled in the history of nations. The stripling youth, young and inexperienced, was now seen contending with the powerful and hard-hearted parent. The rights and the liberties which the God of nature had conferred upon him as his birthright were clandestinely and unfeelingly withheld. The allegorical *David*, unaccustomed to the "tented field," unaccoutred with a coat of mail, and unprovided with an armor-bearer to shield his throbbing breast from the cruel and powerful sword of his enemy, trips forward to meet the *Goliath* of the world, — the lion of the Islands of the seas. The valley that was between them was the vast *Atlantic Ocean;* his armor-bearer was a thousand ships of war, manned by veteran and experienced seamen ; his shield the heavy and thundering artillery, that had so long protected him from the rage of all his foes.

And mark the result ! Relying on the God of armies, his youthful hands prostrated the proud Goliath, and literally killed him with his own sword ; for never could we have conquered the enemy, if we had not taken arms and ammunition wherewith to have taken off his head. We well know that they contended perseveringly, and accomplished the object they had in view. We are enjoying the rich fruits of their labors : may we have the wisdom and virtue to transmit to our posterity unimpaired all these national blessings !

But the "rude din of arms" and "horrors of war" were not all the evils which surrounded our townsmen at this time. To add to the calamities of this (I had almost said ill-fated) town, at the time when the public burdens were the heaviest and most sensibly felt, a powerful religious excitement was produced among the inhabitants, by the preaching and exhortations of one Elder Hix, an itinerant Baptist minister, whose zeal, by what has been related of him, could hardly have been exceeded by St. Paul himself. They went from house to house, convincing

and converting one another; held their meetings by
day and by night, in season and out of season.
Their daily and usual occupations were neglected;
some of the first characters in the town were subjects of irresistible grace, and exhorted and prayed
and admonished each other to flee to the ark of safety; and children and boys, unlearned and untaught,
could pray with the tongues of men and of angels.
Much enthusiasm made them mad, sober reason was
discarded, and the town was well nigh turned upside
down. But listen to the sequel.

When the victims of this delusion (if we may be
allowed so mild an expression) were wrought up to
the highest pitch, when meek-eyed Charity hoped and
believed them to be sincere worshippers of God, the
bubble burst, the wolves in sheep's clothing were discovered. Such a scene of infatuation and corruption
was brought to light as perhaps never was before witnessed in a Christian land. Who could believe that
this monster in sin, though a pretended servant of the
most high God, had long been guilty of conduct that
would disgrace a brothel; and, to fill up the measure
of his iniquity to the brim, he absconded from the town
with a young girl, the miserable dupe of his nefarious
wiles, and a deluded proselyte to his pretended religion. This girl's name was —— Doolittle. As soon
as the rookery was broken up by the arch demon's
decamping, Mr. Amos Marsh cleared out with Mrs.
Doolittle, the girl's mother; and Mr. Amzi Doolittle,
the father of the girl, went off with Mr. Thomas
Barber's wife.

The exasperated friends and relations of some of

these elopers followed after them, and took Mr. Marsh and Mrs. Doolittle somewhere in the State of New York, brought them back, and committed them to jail in Northampton, where they were tried for the crime of adultery, and found guilty. They were sentenced to sit on the gallows, pay a fine, and he was ever after to wear the letter A, in a large capital form, on his outside garment.

Before leaving this disgusting story, I will inform you of one of the methods this famous Elder Hix used to lead astray his credulous hearers, and make them the willing subjects of seduction.

He told them that men and women had their spiritual husbands and wives as well as their temporal; and consequently where the spirit led them to love and admire each other in a spiritual sense, there was no criminality in the connection.

I think we may truly say with the poet, —

> "When such sad scenes our senses pain,
> What eye from weeping can refrain?"

Thus the peace and happiness of four or five families were completely destroyed, and society received an almost irreparable wound. A solemn warning, this, for all of us to beware of impostors, and not to be led away by infatuated religionists, nor deluded by a mistaken zeal.

But to return to our previous subject, respecting the national difficulties and obstacles that our fathers encountered in those exciting and trying times.

Our government was only a rope of sand. A new

constitution for the Commonwealth of Massachusetts had been drawn up and submitted to the town for their approbation or disapproval; and it was almost unanimously opposed, only three voting in favor of it. The proposed constitution did not agree with their liberal and republican principles; yet, at the same meeting, they voted to grant the requisition of the General Court, respecting supplying their proportion towards clothing the Continental army.

The town at this time was also destitute of a minister; the Rev. Lemuel Hedge having died Oct. 17, 1777, on the very day that Gen. Burgoyne surrendered his army to the Americans.

The depreciation in the paper money then in circulation was an evil severely felt: silver and gold was scarce, and the circulating medium was principally paper. For an example of its value, it is recorded that at the annual meeting in March, 1779, eight hundred pounds was raised to repair the highways, two-thirds of it to be laid out on the county road; and the wages of a man was fixed at thirty-six shillings per day, and a yoke of oxen at three dollars.

The December previous (1778), it was voted to give the Rev. Samuel Reed six hundred and seventy-five pounds, as a settlement in the gospel ministry; and it was also voted to relinquish all that are not of the Congregational denomination from paying ministerial charges.

They also voted to pay the Rev. Samuel Reed sixty pounds lawful money for the first year's salary, and seventy pounds a year afterwards; said salary to be paid in money, equal to rye at three shillings and sixpence per bushel, and corn at two shillings and eight-pence per bushel. Rev. Samuel Reed was ordained in Warwick, Sept. 23, 1779, and he had thirty cords of wood added to his salary annually.

The town meetings at this time were called in the name and government of the people of the State of Massachusetts Bay. In June, 1779, the town convened for the purpose of petitioning the General Court to relinquish a heavy fine laid on them for not raising their quota of men, and to represent their inability to raise men for the service in proportion to their numbers. It has been said that the town could not procure men without paying large bounties, or providing for their families while they were absent; a large proportion of the inhabitants being poor.

The town chose a committee of five to draft a petition out of two forms produced by Lieut. Thomas Rich and Col. Samuel Williams, which was to be signed by the town clerk in behalf of the town, for a redress of grievances. In August, 1779, the town voted ' to warn out all persons residing in said town, that were not inhabitants," according to law ; and for the future to practise accordingly. They also voted to send a member to the county convention, to be holden at Northampton, to state the prices of the necessaries of life. Lieut. Josiah Pomeroy was chosen. After the delegate had returned from Northampton, the town voted to adopt the doings of the convention, and chose a committee of seven persons to fix the price of hay and other articles which should be thought proper. They also chose a committee of three persons to hear complaints, provided that any should transgress these regulations.

On the 8th of November, the town voted to raise seven hundred pounds to pay bounties and mileage of soldiers.

1780.

This year the paper money had so depreciated, that five thousand pounds was voted to repair the highways. Men's wages fixed at nine pounds per day, and a yoke of oxen five pounds, and a cart or plough at three pounds per day; and fifteen hundred pounds was raised for the support of the poor.

May 17, this year, the sixth article in the warrant is as follows: viz., "To see if the town will take any method to prevent the wolves catching sheep."

The present constitution of this State was laid before 'the town for their acceptance the twenty-fourth day of May of this year; and they voted to accept the third article, viz., " the article on religious freedom:" seventy-three voting in favor of the article, and finally the whole constitution at large, with this amendment: viz., "That no person shall hold a seat in the civil department of government, except he be a professor of the Christian Protestant religion." Afterwards it was voted not to receive the constitution with the proposed amendment; and a committee was chosen to regulate the objections and amendments.

The town was called on, in June, to raise a number of men for six months; and a committee was chosen, with instructions to offer the men that would go into the service for that time fifteen pounds bounty, equal to silver or gold, or a sum equal to their wages. In

July following, the town raised fourteen hundred and forty-nine pounds and twelve shillings, to pay said bounty; and they also raised five thousand pounds for defraying necessary charges; and in September, to cap the whole, they voted to raise twenty thousand pounds to pay up the soldiers.

1781.

Jan. 8, the town voted three thousand one hundred pounds, to pay for horses for the Continental service. About this time the town was called on for three years' men; and they voted to class the town, and each class was to provide a man, and pay him. Thus may be readily perceived the difficulties that beset our townsmen. We ought to feel grateful that Providence has cast our lot in an age that is distinguished for peace and prosperity, and that we have none to molest us or make us afraid. But the story of our predecessors' sufferings is not yet all told.

This town was called upon, in July, to raise seven militiamen, and a quantity of beef for the use of the army; and the town raised, or voted to raise, sixty pounds, silver money, to pay for said beef. And also chose a committee of three men to give them their own securities, and the town would indemnify the committee. They also raised thirty pounds lawful money to pay the men a part of their wages.

Is it not a matter of astonishment how this town, poor and oppressed as it was with the public burdens of those times, ever succeeded in defraying them, without leaving a large debt for their posterity to cancel? But it appears that they did. They must have been better economists than we are, or it never could have been done. In the midst of all their poverty and privations, they seemed to be looking forward into futurity, and making calculations for after-ages, as well as for their own convenience.

In September of this year, they called a town meeting, and chose a committee of three to petition the General Court to set off the north-west part of the county of Worcester, and the north-east part of Hampshire, into a separate county. Here follows the petition : —

"At a town-meeting held in Warwick, Sept. 19, 1781, taking into consideration the many hardships and disadvantages incident to individuals, as well as towns and places, when their situation is remote from county administration. Such is the case with this town, that the inhabitants cannot make any title to their lands without going sixty miles to get their deeds recorded ; and all probate business, as well as other county matters, are finished at a great distance. Which burden, in addition to our proportion in the common cause, renders the inhabitants of this town, and others in like circumstances, unable to continue their exertions with the people and towns who are at little or no expense to do such business."

The committee were instructed to write to the towns of Hardwick, Barre, Hubbardston, Templeton, Winchendon, Petersham, Athol, and Royalston, in the county of Worcester ; and to Greenwich, New Salem, Shutesbury, Wendell, and Erving's Grant, and such other towns as they shall think proper, to unite with them in petitioning the General Court to accomplish their object; also to meet delegates from those towns at Samuel Peckham's tavern in Petersham, on the sixth day of November following, at ten o'clock, A.M., to consult on the best method of proceeding.

In October this year, the town voted to set off four thousand and sixty acres of land (as exhibited on a plan shown by Elijah Ball), with the inhabitants on the same, to be incorporated into a town with other lands from Athol, Royalston, and Erving's Grant. This town was called Orange.

1782.

In 1782, Mr. Moses Leonard gave the town what is now the north part of the burying-ground, on condition that the town will fence the same with a good fence fronting the road, with posts and two rails and a suitable wall under the same; he reserving the privilege of feeding the same with neat cattle and sheep only.

Many of the bodies of the dead were dug up, and removed by their friends from the first burial ground to the present place of interment.

At the May meeting this year, Capt. John Goldsbury was chosen representative, and a committee was chosen to draw instructions for the representative, to be laid before the town for their approbation; and the meeting was adjourned until the next Thursday, to hear them. They are as follows, viz.:—

To Capt. John Goldsbury, —

Sir, — You being chosen to represent us in the General Court of this Commonwealth, we, the inhabitants of the town of Warwick, do give you the following instructions: viz., That you do your endeavor that the sums apportioned on us of the public charges be lessened, as we think that they are more than our part, according to our ability. That the governor, council, senate, and all other men in this State that are under public pay, be lessened to a reasonable rate. That the charges annually arising be ascertained. That you inquire into the state of the treasury, and of what money hath been granted, and how applied. That all men unnecessarily employed in public business be dismissed. That the General Court be removed out of Boston into some other town."

These instructions have been copied as a specimen of the fashion of the times; and also hoping, that, from these blunt hints, those now in public business might gather some instruction from it.

1783.

The north and north-west part of the town (viz. school districts, Nos. 7, 8, and 10, as they now are) were divided in 1783, and the line between them was as follows: viz., "The line to be from what is called Bennett's Knob, Mount Grace, and to extend to Jonathan Smith's south-west corner, and to extend in a straight line to said Smith's south-east corner, and thence northerly the same point to the State-line."

At the May meeting this year, it was voted that the

"Selectmen be directed to write in their returns to the General Court, that, considering the extreme poverty of the town, they have not chosen a representative the present year."

June 23 of this year, in town-meeting, it was voted "That the new plantation (Orange) called South Warwick be districted to the town of Warwick, with the privilege of joining with us in the choice of a representative, but to act with us in no town affairs whatever."

1784.

On the 20th of January, the town chose Thomas Rich and Capt. Peter Proctor, a committee to assist the selectmen in procuring the best account of the charges that have arisen during the war. (No report found.)

On the 3d of May, the district of Orange was summoned for the first time to meet with the town of Warwick to choose a representative; and Dea. James Ball was chosen. This year we find an account exhibited by Mr. Isaac Hastings, which at this day would appear novel; viz., "To taking care of the meeting-house and mending the doors, eight shillings. To making a tythingman's club and a warden's staff, two shillings." (The account was allowed.)

1785.

This year the town was divided into nine school-districts by a committee, who named the inhabitants that should belong to each; and in this imperfect manner they have remained ever since, excepting some small alteration, and a division of the north-west district, making ten in the whole.

In August a meeting was called to see what the town would do with William Houghton's rates; and it was "voted that the selectmen be chosen to inspect and oversee William Houghton, and see that the produce of his labor be appropriated towards paying his taxes as far as may be; and if the produce of his labor finally fails, and his taxes cannot be recovered, the town shall indemnify the constables respecting his taxes."

1786.

In 1786, the inhabitants met in town-meeting, and chose Capt. John Goldsbury as a suitable person to be commissioned as a justice of the peace, and forwarded a petition to the governor, in recommendation of him. A minority of the voters protested against the proceedings, declaring that a justice of the peace could not be chosen by the town constitutionally.

About this time the public mind was considerably agitated by a rebellion of a part of the good citizens of Massachusetts. The insurgents, with one Daniel Shays, a native of Pelham, at their head, threatened to break up the government of the State, and to put down all the authority of its members. They actually assembled a considerable force; and for a while they increased in numbers to such a degree as actually to spread terror and dismay through the Commonwealth.

The government raised a large body of men to quell them, and several lives were lost before they were brought to terms. This town did not escape the shock, being considerably divided. Some espoused the cause of the rebels; while others stood by their rulers.

Several town-meetings were called; they chose a delegate to send to a convention in Hatfield, to devise means to allay the disturbance. Mr. Jacob Packard was the delegate chosen. They called a town-meeting to see if the town would assist the selectmen, they having been imprisoned for acting in their office. But the article was passed over.

In September, 1786, there is an agreement with Capt. Samuel Langley to build a new meeting-house recorded as follows, viz. : —

"The house to be fifty-eight feet long and forty-two feet wide, with a porch on the front of the house, sufficient to contain convenient stairs to go up into the galleries. There is to be forty pews on the lower floor (agreeable to a plan herewith exhibited); there is to be galleries in the front, and at each end of the house, fourteen feet wide from the wall, with pews on the back of said galleries, five feet eight inches wide from the wall; the rest of the gallery to be seats with a convenient alley round, agreeable to a plan herewith submitted. The seats in the front gallery to be for singers to sit in; the seats in the side galleries to be for persons to sit in, as the Congregational Society shall direct. The house to be completely finished off by the first day of September, 1788, in the following form and manner: viz., The pews to be with wainscot work, with frieze panels or banisters, and one seat in each pew. The front of the body-seats and the deacons' seat to be wainscot-work, with a convenient communion-table. The body-seats on the lower floor, and the seats in the gallery, to be all framed. The pulpit to be built after the Doric order, with fluted pillars, and architraves by the sides of the window. The bottom of the canopy to be an octagon panel in the centre. The remaining part by the same rule, the top to be turned with an O. G.; the entablature to be by the Corinthian order, except the modillion; the breast-work of the galleries to be one wide panel with dental cornices, and built with six turned pillars under the galleries, and panel pillars over the same on the breast-work. One eight-panel door at each end of the house, with pediments and double architraves. One double door and two single doors to the porch, with architraves, cornice, and caps; double doors with six panels each at the entrance of the house, out of the porch, above and below. The frame to be as follows: The sills to be of yellow pine, nine by ten inches square. Five lower summers to be twelve inches square. Four corner posts ten inches square; to be oak, with cock tenons. Eight pine cock-tenon posts ten inches square. Four prick posts ten inches square. Eight pair of rafters nine by ten inches square. Six pair of compass rafters. Four kingposts broad studded, twelve inches over on each side; the joists in the lower floor to be within two feet of each other, and those in the roof to be three feet from each other. The house to be braced up and down, in every place where the windows and doors will admit. The boards on the roof to be jointed. The roof to be shingled with good fifteen-inch shingles, with double cornice at the gable ends, with one compass window in each gable end; thirty-three windows in the body of the house, of twenty-four squares in each window of eight by ten London crown or Bristol glass, with good frames, cornice, and solid caps; and one window in the porch of the house; and the porch to be clapboarded with good sound clapboards planed. The floor to be double, the upper floor to be jointed, the pew floors to be jointed and planed. The gallery floor to be double. The ceiling over the body of the house and under the galleries, and the walls (except the board ceiling from the floors), to be lathed and plastered. The house and porch to be well underpinned with good stones.

"And the said Samuel Langley do hereby promise and engage to build the house, and finish it off workmanlike, agreeable to the foregoing directions, by the time before mentioned, on the following conditions: viz., That a sufficient number of the society appear to purchase thirty-nine pews on the lower floor (the pew next adjoining the pulpit stairs to be for the use of the Congregational minister for the time being), the said thirty-nine pews to be nine pounds each on an average, and to be paid for in the following manner: viz., Two pounds in cash for each pew when the meeting-house is raised; two pounds more for each pew when they are finished off; the rest of the pay for each pew to be paid for in neat cattle, sheep, or flax-seed, at the current price when the meeting-house is completely finished. The pews in the gallery to be five pounds each, on an average, to all such persons that return their names to the committee to become purchasers by the fifth day of October next. After that day any person may purchase any of the pews in the gallery of the said Langley, as he and they can agree; as those pews are to be his property till sold. The body seats on the lower floor to be used and improved by any persons that shall choose to occupy them, as the Congregational Society shall order. And I, the said Samuel Langley, do further agree and engage that I will receive of the purchasers of the forementioned pews, towards pay for the same, the following materials, at the prices fixed to each article, of each man's proportion as it shall be apportioned by the Society's committee, if each person shall give notice to the committee by the first day of November next that they will provide their said proportion of the materials at the spot by the time hereafter prefixed. And if any person shall neglect to notify the committee as aforesaid, he forfeits his chance of paying in such materials, and the committee may employ any other of the purchasers of pews as they shall think just; so that there may be no failure of the materials being all on the spot by the time hereafter mentioned. The materials are as follows: viz., Ten thousand of good ceiling-boards, one inch and one-eighth thick, at one pound, ten shillings. Twenty-five thousand good merchantable inch boards, at one pound, five shillings. Five thousand half-inch pine boards, at one pound. Nine thousand half-inch chestnut boards, at one pound. Eight thousand of good sawed clapboards, six inches wide, at one pound, five shillings. Twenty-nine thousand of good fifteen-inch shingles, at eight shillings per thousand. One hundred pieces of slit-work fourteen feet long, four by five inches, at the rate of twenty-eight shillings per thousand. Eighty pieces fourteen feet long, four by five, at twenty-six shillings per thousand. Thirty pieces twelve feet long, four by four, twenty-six shillings per thousand. Sixty pieces, nine feet long, three by five, same price. Ten hogsheads of good stone lime, at two pounds, fourteen shillings, per hogshead. And if any of the proprietors of pews shall see fit to pay any of the following articles at the prices thereto affixed, towards paying for their pews, I will receive the same, and receipt on delivery, and receive their receipt in pay for their pews. The articles are as follows: viz., Six thousand of double tens at thirteen shillings per thousand. Thirty thousand tenpenny nails, at nine shillings per thousand. Ninety-four thousand fourpenny nails, at three shillings and four pence per thousand. Five thousand of fivepenny brads, at six shillings per thousand. Three thousand of threepenny brads, at three shillings per thousand. Sixty-two pair of pew-door hinges, at one shilling and four pence per pair. Six boxes of London crown or Bristol glass, eight by ten size, at five pounds, two shillings, per hundred feet. The pews in the gallery that are purchased by the first day of October next to be paid for in the following manner: viz., One dollar in cash when the meeting-house is raised, and one dollar more when the pews are finished; the next to be paid in neat stock, sheep, or flax-seed, when the meeting-house is completely finished. The slit-work to be at the spot by the first day of May next. The boards, shingles, and clapboards, by the first day of June next. The lime by the first day of September next.

"And I, the said Samuel Langley, do further agree and promise, that if there should be any donations in labor or in any other way given towards the meeting-house, that I will render an account to the committee of the same, towards the pay of the thirty-nine pews on the lower floor, and in the gallery, as it shall be apportioned by the committee.

"And I, the said Samuel Langley, do agree that the committee shall inspect and view the workmanship and materials of the meeting-house when finished; and if they judge that there is any deficiency in the work or materials, that I will leave the matter out to disinterested persons that understand such business, that the committee and I shall mutually choose; and I will oblige myself to abide their judgment. "As witness my hand,

"SAMUEL LANGLEY.

"WARWICK, Sept. 15, 1786."

And further respecting the meeting-house, it was first decided to face it to the west; but afterwards it was agreed to face it to the south, as it now stands.

A meeting was called in August, to hear the petition of James Ball respecting the meeting-house, which is as follows : viz., To see if the town will vote to take the windows that are in the old meeting-house in Warwick, and divide them equally among the school-districts proportionally as the school-wards stand on the town invoice ; and also proceed to sell the old meeting-house for what it will fetch at vendue, and the money or securities arising by the sale of said old meeting-house, bring into the town treasury of Warwick, to defray the public charges of the town, or otherwise dispose of the said meeting-house as the town shall see fit, on condition the petitioners produce to the town an agreement or vote of the Congregational Society in Warwick, that all persons of any denomination of Christians in Warwick may and shall have free liberty to meet with the said Congregational Society on the Lord's days and other times, for public worship in the new meeting-house ; and that the town may and shall have the same right to meet in the new meeting-house in Warwick at all times hereafter, to transact the town's public business, as the town now has in the old meeting-house.

At this meeting it was proposed, whether the town would give the old meeting-house to the proprietors of the new one, on condition that the Society give to the town of Warwick a good deed of all the privileges in the new meeting-house, agreeable to a vote of the Society ; and this vote passed in the affirmative.

At this meeting the selectmen were chosen a committee to receive the deed for the town from the Society.

It appears that Capt. Langley built the above-mentioned meeting-house, by the job, for the sum of fifteen hundred dollars ; and the thirty-nine pews on the lower floor at nine pounds each, and twenty pews in the gallery at five pounds each, make but a trifle over this sum. The pews were called equal in value ; and the members of the society *cast lots* for the first choice on the lower floor. Old Mr. Thomas Gould got the first choice ; and he chose the pew where Mr. Elijah Fisk now sits, on the right-hand side of the broad aisle near the centre of the house. Mr. Moses Fay had the last choice, — " Hobson's choice," — that or none ; and he had the south-west corner pew. Capt. Langley made a losing job, as he had the gallery pews at five pounds each ; and they were not all sold for many years, and then at a very low price ; and his loss was increased by his losing his dwelling-house, with the principal part of his furniture, by fire ; and he had almost finished all the pews and doors for the meeting-house, which were all thus suddenly consumed. The Society made him some remuneration, but not enough to compensate his loss.

1787.

In March, 1787, the town assembled as usual, and, for some cause now unknown, adjourned the meeting until April ; and at this meeting it was insisted on, that the meeting should be regulated according to an act of the General Court, published in February, 1786. Whereupon the selectmen and assessors exhibited a list of voters, which was read ; and, after some debate, it was moved that a vote should be taken, whether the town would proceed ; and it passed in the affirmative. And the records say, that " Maj. Joseph Mayo protested against the meeting." This transaction is noted, because it was the first time a list of voters was read in town-meeting in this place, and also to show the propensity of mankind to oppose and object to every thing new, right or wrong. The assessors' account for the last year's service was allowed, it being only one pound, twelve shillings, each. At the close of the record of this meeting, it is stated, "That the above chosen officers *in general* have taken their respective oaths." " The officers required by law have taken and subscribed the oath of allegiance."

A meeting was called in August to choose a constable ; and the fourth article in the warrant is here noted for its novelty ; viz., " To hear *any request* of the inhabitants of the town of Warwick, or act any thing thereon as the town shall think proper." This article must have been broad enough to have satisfied the most querulous and gainsaying without any additional words. But the article was passed over.

Another meeting was called in October, one article of which was to see if the town will assist the selectmen in their being taken and imprisoned in May last for acting in their office, and to prosecute those persons that took them, or act any thing on that matter that the town shall think proper ; and choose attorney or attorneys to carry on the same, as the town shall think fit. Josiah Cobb, Thomas Rich, and James Goldsbury, were the selectmen ; and I have never been able to find out the particulars of this affair of imprisonment, but suppose it originated in transactions in the Shays Rebellion. The town, however, passed the article over.

In March, 1789, we have the first record of perambulating the town-lines. That part of the line between Warwick and Orange was perambulated Dec. 26, 1788, by James Goldsbury and Mark Moore for Warwick, and Levi Cheney and Joseph Metcalf for Orange; and their report not agreeing with the act of incorporation of Orange, is the original source of the difficulty that now exists between the towns, respecting the lines between them. Capt. John Goldsbury was chosen representative to Court.

1790.

In March, 1790, the town voted fifteen pounds for the support of the poor. They also voted, and chose Josiah Cobb, James Goldsbury, and Samuel Langley, a committee to stake out suitable places on the meeting-house common, for people to build noon-houses and stables on, if requested by the inhabitants.

John Goldsbury, Esq., was chosen representative for Warwick and Orange. He was also chosen in 1791 and 1792. In 1791 an attempt was made to form a new county, by joining with a part of Worcester County. It was voted this year that the school-money be divided according to the number of scholars in the several wards, and the selectmen directed to number the scholars in each ward.

It appears that the Rev. Samuel Reed had been supported by a fund for a number of years. This fund was created in the following manner: Each individual that meant to support him gave a note to a committee appointed to receive them, of the amount he was willing to put in; which several notes, bearing interest at six per cent, constituted the fund, the interest of which paid the salary, so that each man's interest on his note was his minister-tax. In August this year, it was voted unanimously, that it was their minds that the fund that was raised in Warwick for the support of a Congregational minister ought to be dissolved, on condition and agreeable to the petition of Ezra Conant and others, and for the future a gospel minister be supported agreeable to the Constitution of this Commonwealth. The aforesaid fund had been legally incorporated; and Mr. Ezra Conant's petition was one that had been presented to the General Court to repeal the fund act. It had had a hearing, and an order of notice had been served on the town, to give them a chance to object against the repeal of the act if they thought proper.

In November, 1792, the town voted for electors of president and vice-president for the first time, an act of the General Court having authorized them to do so at the June session previous.

1793.

At the annual meeting this year, there was but five pounds raised for the support of the poor.

John Goldsbury, Esq., was chosen representative.

This year a committee was raised by the town to look up the school and ministry rights of land, and to see what had been done respecting the sale of them. They reported, May 6, at an adjourned meeting, that two hundred and ninety-one acres of the school-land had been sold for one hundred and twenty-eight pounds, fourteen shillings. Lot No. 26, in the fifth division, containing fourteen acres, not sold. Also that three hundred and five acres of the ministry-land had been sold for two hundred and thirty-nine pounds.

This is the source from which the town now receives interest-money to help support the minister and schools. The interest we receive annually towards supporting the minister is fifty-four dollars; and each of the ten school-districts draws three dollars annually from the school-fund, making thirty dollars.

This year the town voted that each school-district should draw what money it pays. At a subsequent meeting, they voted that Mr. Jonathan Gale be empowered to provide a funeral carriage. Also voted, and chose Dea. James Ball, Capt. Mark Moore, and Lieut. Jonathan Gale, a committee to divide the town, and establish a line between the two militia companies. Previous to this, there had been two companies; but every soldier, when he became liable to do military duty, had his choice which company to join. This practice gave rise to some unpleasant feelings; as, each captain or commanding officer being anxious to secure the new recruits, means were sometimes resorted to which could not be justified by gentlemen of honor.

But this intangible line had the same effect that the stupendous Chinese wall had in another case; and the competition ceased. The old north road to Northfield, and the road to Royalston, by Caleb Mayo's, each leading from the meeting-house, was the line established. In October, the town was convened to choose a delegate to meet a Court's committee at Asahel Pomeroy's, in Northampton, respecting a division of the County of Hampshire. John Goldsbury, Esq., was chosen, and instructed to oppose the division, stating that they considered it would be detrimental to the town and the county at large.

1794.

This year John Goldsbury, Esq., was again chosen representative. Eight pounds, three shillings, were voted to pay Jonathan Gale for the funeral carriage. It was also voted to build a house for said carriage; which was put up at auction, and struck off to David Mayo for five pounds, two shillings. This year the town chose a committee, consisting of Mark Moore, Caleb Mayo, and Abraham Gale, to invite the Rev. Samuel Reed to extend the relation subsisting between him and the Congregational Society in Warwick to the town, so that he might be the town's minister, instead of the Society's, upon the town's agreeing to pay him his salary; with a proviso, that all persons of other denominations were to be exempted from taxation for ministerial purposes. The town then agreed to pay him seventy pounds in silver, at six shillings and eight pence per ounce, and twenty cords of merchantable wood yearly, and every year, so long as he shall remain their minister. And they also voted, that he should have the money that the ministry-lots of land were sold for, by giving good security therefor, and deducting the interest out of his salary yearly.

The Rev. Samuel Reed returned the following answer: —

"GENTLEMEN, — I have received by your committee the explanation of your grant of my salary, and also the additional grant of the improvement of the ministry money on the mentioned conditions, and am happy in the confidence I find, after so long a connection and acquaintance, you still place in me. And now I freely, and agreeably to your request, extend my ministerial relation to all the Congregational inhabitants of the town of Warwick, and will endeavor faithfully to discharge my trust, as far as my many imperfections will admit, charitably trusting that I shall meet with that friendship and candor which is so absolutely necessary for enjoyment and happiness in such a relation. My friends, if we all study those things that make for peace, we shall gain the invaluable Pearl; and the God of love and peace who has so long propitiously beheld this church, we may humbly hope, will grant that we still rejoice under his smiles; and on his wisdom and goodness may we constantly rely, in humble and cheerful obedience to his will. May his grace be sufficient for us, to lead, protect, and defend us in this militant state; may we grow in knowledge and every Christian virtue, and finally come to the stature of perfect men in Christ, and be thought worthy to join his church above!

"To this our great God and King, and to the mercy of his

grace, I commend you, and desire to be commended by you; and under him, and depending on his promises, I subscribe myself your sincere and humble servant,

"SAMUEL REED.

"Nov. 3, 1794."

Mr. Reed's salary was to commence at the above date. The town chose a committee, consisting of Rev. Samuel Reed, John Goldsbury, Esq., and Capt. Mark Moore, to petition the General Court to repeal the act whereby the Congregational Society in Warwick was incorporated, and a fund raised, for the support of the gospel ministry.

1795.

This year there was a town-meeting, called to collect the sentiments of the town on the expediency of amending the Constitution. Twenty-one voted in favor of amendment, and nineteen against it. John Goldsbury, Esq., was chosen representative. On May 11 the town empowered the selectmen to lease out that part of the Common west of the road, for any term of time not exceeding twenty years. They also empowered them to exchange lands with Josiah Pomeroy, jun., in order to straighten the line between the said town and the said Pomeroy.

The town granted twenty dollars to erect guide-posts, — the first that had been erected by law. They also reconsidered a former vote to build a stone pound, and voted to build one of wood; said pound was to be thirty feet square, and well framed, and handsomely underpinned with stones ; the sills to be eight by ten inches square, the rails to be three by five inches, and the plates six by seven inches square ; and it was put up at auction to the lowest bidder, and struck off to Gilbert Mellen for thirteen dollars and eighty-three cents.

1796.

In April the town voted that the selectmen be a committee to sell school-lot No. 26, at the adjournment of the meeting. Nathaniel Cheney (of Orange) represented the district.

1797.

It was voted to raise thirty pounds for killing wildcats the year past, and to continue the bounty, at twenty shillings per head, the coming year.

The town allowed the assessors for taking the invoice and assessing the taxes in 1796, ten days, at eighty cents per day. Considerable difficulty existed in the town about this time, in regard to the school districts. The districts No. 2 and No. 3 had been joined together, and afterwards separated. They could not agree where to build the schoolhouse in No. 2 ; and the town voted and chose Dea. Chamberlain of Winchester, Maj. Alexander of Northfield, and Oliver Chapin of Orange, to decide the dispute, and assign the spot to build upon, the district to pay the expense. Oliver Chapin was chosen representative.

The town voted one hundred dollars in addition to the Rev. Samuel Reed's salary.

1798.

William Heath had fifty-eight votes for governor, and fifty-seven for lieutenant-governor.

Josiah Cobb was chosen representative.

The Rev. Samuel Reed considering that the town did not support him agreeable to their first contract, requested an article to be inserted in the warrant to dismiss him from the ministry; but, on the particular request of his friends, he had the article withdrawn.

Nov. 5, this year, it was voted to discharge the tax on dogs by one day's work on the highways for each dog; and that they fetch a certificate from the highway surveyor under whom they work to the selectmen, certifying that the services are done.

1799.

A committee was chosen to look into the situation of the school districts; and they reported to have the town divided into seven districts, and each one to draw an equal share of the school-money. They also voted and chose a committee to appraise the schoolhouses, and another to see what articles are necessary for building new schoolhouses, and to put up the stuff at vendue, and the work also.

It was afterwards voted to have the districts remain as they were; viz., that there should be nine.

Oliver Chapin was chosen representative.

1800.

The town voted not to choose a representative this year.

1801.

It was voted to raise four hundred dollars to pay for preaching, and each denomination to draw what they pay.

1802.

Josiah Cobb was chosen representative.

A committee was raised, consisting of Mark Moore, Peter Proctor, Josiah Pomeroy, Jacob Rich, Caleb Mayo, Asa Conant, and Ebenezer Williams, to look into the state of the treasury, and to make a report what sums there are that belong to the ministry, and what other unappropriated moneys were to be found there. The committee subsequently reported that there was $1,222.85; that $796.67 had been received from the sales of the ministerial lands, and $499 from the sale of the school-lands; that there was $332.85 of unappropriated money in the treasury, besides Mr. Hedge's donation, which amounted to $93.33. This donation, as we have been informed, was from Mr. Elisha Hedge, the father of Rev. Lemuel Hedge, our first minister. We have never learned the amount of this gift, but have found in the old Congregational society's records, that a committee was chosen, consisting of Dea. James Ball, Col. Samuel Williams, and Joseph

Mayo, to send a letter of thanks to Mr. Hedge for his generous donation towards the fund. This was the 12th of August, 1779. The presumption is, that it was a sum that, with the interest added, after the dissolution of the fund to the time of this report, which is dated March 31, 1803, would amount to $93.33.

The committee reported that there was a deficiency of the money that the ministry and school lands sold for of $166.15. The town voted to raise the last-mentioned sum, and to have it placed on interest, and to be applied annually for the use of schooling. Here terminates the continual strife and fluctuation of our funds in this town; and from this date we may consider them settled, permanent, and secure, amounting to $1,383.

1805.

In 1805 a town-meeting was called, to hear a circular letter, respecting dividing the county of Hampshire; and Caleb Mayo was chosen an agent, to meet other agents at Greenfield to petition the General Court for said division. The division was not effected at this time; but the subject was frequently agitated: and in November, 1810, Justus Russell, Esq., was chosen agent for the town; and the final division was consummated in 1812.

In 1805 the town was, perhaps, as much divided on political matters as at any period since its first settlement. Federalists and Democrats were the assumed names of the parties; and the contention ran so high, that fathers, children, brothers, kinsmen, and fellow-townsmen, when convened to exercise the elective franchise, appeared more like angry contending foes, marshalled in battle-array, than like freemen and fellow-citizens. There was no neutral ground. Each party had for its motto, "He that is not for us is against us." The regulations of the law made it necessary, that, to be a voter in the choice of a representative, you "must be a resident in the town for the space of one year next preceding, and have a freehold estate within the town of the annual income of ten dollars, or any estate to the value of two hundred dollars." Very few were to be found that could not show two hundred dollars' worth of property on the day of election, when perhaps the day before, or the day after, you could not collect a just debt of five dollars. The aged, the lame, and the sick were alike compelled "to come in," to swell and strengthen the one, or to overpower the opposing party. The parties were almost equally balanced here : while the district of Orange was united with us in the choice of a representative ; and they were as divided, as acrimonious, and as uncompromising, as we were. At the May meeting this year, the inhabitants of Warwick and Orange assembled to choose a representative. All Yankees are naturally jealous of their rights and liberty, but rendered doubly so by the impulse of party feelings, — each party distrustful of the other, and each determined to gain the ascendency, and carry the vote. The presiding officers, for the time being, were critically situated ; and, do right or do wrong, bitter imprecations fell on their devoted heads.

The jealousy and distrust ran so high, that they agreed to leave the meeting-house, and go out upon the Common, each party with their respective leaders: accordingly they marched out in Indian file, and paraded in two parallel lines, so that each, being single, might put in his vote without a chance for deception, or of voting twice; and each might be counted, viz. the number of voters, and the number of votes given in. The town-clerk and selectmen carried the ballot-boxes to the voters. The candidates at this election were Caleb Mayo, Esq., Federal; and Ebenezer Williams, Esq., Democratic. On ascertaining the number of votes, E. Williams, Esq., had one hundred and forty-eight, and C. Mayo, Esq., had one hundred and fifty-four, and was chosen. The language and looks and gestures of the contending parties this day, the pen of a *Milton*, perhaps, could have adequately described; but mine would fail in the attempt.

1806.

In 1806 Caleb Mayo, Esq., and Josiah Cobb Esq., were the opposing candidates, and Esquire Cobb was chosen. For the benefit of future generations, I have now recited some of the principal incidents in this regularly fought battle of the contending political parties, presuming that no other record of it is now extant, excepting in the memories of our fathers and fellow-townsmen, which will soon be lost forever.

Voted to repair the meeting-house, and to accept of the request of Caleb Mayo and others for the town to relinquish their right and privilege, granted them by the proprietors, of two of the back seats on each side of the broad aisle on the lower floor, and fourteen feet of the seats at the north end of each of the side galleries in said meeting-house, so as to enable the proprietors to erect four pews on the lower and four pews in the gallery of equal size of the other pews in said house, the sale of which to defray a part of the expense of repairing and painting said house. These petitioners were Caleb Mayo, Abraham Stevens, Daniel Whitney, Jonathan Blake, Nathaniel G. Stevens, Benjamin Conant, Josiah Smith, Ebenezer Williams, Zachariah Barber, and John Gale.

Caleb Mayo, Esq., William Cobb, jun., and Perez Allen, were chosen a committee to superintend the repairing of the meeting-house. In December the town voted their consent that the Baptist society, which was partly in Warwick and partly in Royalston, should be incorporated.

1807.

The town voted two hundred dollars to pay for repairing the meeting-house.

1808.

This year the town of Warwick and the district of Orange voted to send two representatives; and chose Ebenezer Williams, Esq., and Josiah Cobb, Esq. (both

Democrats). The militia companies of this town were called to Hadley to a division-muster this year; and the town voted to pay the officers and soldiers that should attend said muster one dollar each from the treasury. Also the town voted to concur with the town of Boston in preferring a memorial to the President of the United States for the repeal of the embargo, and chose Caleb Mayo, Josiah Pomeroy, Josiah Proctor, Jonathan Blake, jun., and Justus Russell, a committee to prepare a memorial, and adjourned the meeting half an hour. On the meeting being opened, the following petition was accepted unanimously : —

To his Excellency Thomas Jefferson, President of the United States.

The petition of the inhabitants of the town of Warwick, in the County of Hampshire and Commonwealth of Massachusetts, in legal town meeting assembled, beg leave to represent: That the inconveniences and privations of property already experienced in consequence of the embargo on the vessels and export-trade of the United States fill them with serious apprehensions for the evils that must necessarily result from a prohibition of the exports of the surplus produce of the present season.

They sincerely regret the necessity (if such existed) of the laws laying an embargo on the extensive navigation of the United States, and prohibiting internal intercourse. By the first, the commercial enterprise of the New-England States, that secured to the farmer a sure market and high price for his produce, is wholly destroyed; and the grievous privations occasioned by the latter have produced in some of the less patriotic sufferers a relaxation of principles, and a contempt for the laws, more to be deplored than the loss of property, and more to be feared from its consequences than from the hostility of any nation whatever. That professing a firm attachment to the constitution of government, under which they have enjoyed unexampled prosperity and happiness, they have in all respects observed a due submission to the embargo laws, and measures of your administration, however · distressing or unequal their operation, and impressed at all times with the feelings and sentiments of freemen, and jealous of their rights as independent Republicans, will ever stand ready with their lives and fortunes to support the constituted authorities of their country, whenever it is necessary for the defence of those rights and privileges so essential to the happiness of the United States, and of which they claim an equal share. They regret the necessity they are under of calling the particular attention of your Excellency to their relief; but are happy in the enjoyment of the privilege of peaceably and respectfully petitioning for a redress of grievances, whenever they exist. And as our national legislature, contemplating a change of circumstances that might render the embargo unnecessary, have vested in you the power of suspending its operations, and humbly conceiving that such a change has taken place as will justify the measure, they have a full confidence in your early attention to the true interests of your country, and the suffering of its citizens.

Your petitioners therefore pray your Excellency, in pursuance of the aforesaid power, to suspend the operations of the embargo, in whole or in part, as your superior wisdom shall direct, and as in duty bound shall ever pray.

Which was signed by the aforesaid committee.

It was then voted that the selectmen sign the petition, and transmit it to the President of the United States.

1812.

This year it was voted that the selectmen procure a funeral hearse with four wheels (the former funeral carriage had but two); and it was voted to raise fifty dollars to pay for the same.*

On the thirty-first day of July, 1812, Rev. Samuel Reed died, aged fifty-seven years, having been minister in the town nearly thirty-three years. In September the town voted two hundred dollars to defray his funeral expenses, and to procure preaching the remainder of the year; and chose Caleb Mayo, Ebenezer Pierce, Samuel Ball, Justus Russell, and William Cobb, a committee to provide some person or persons to supply the pulpit until the next annual meeting.

I will here record as a matter of history a brief account of the Franklin Glass-Factory Company's proceedings in this town, with the rise and origin of that presumptuous adventure, its short but momentous life, its premature and lamented death.

This year Dr. Ebenezer Hall, an inhabitant and practising physician in this town, possessing a considerable share of natural powers of mind, and a peculiarly fascinating and alluring address, more brilliant than solid, more theoretical and visionary than practical and real, conceived the idea that he could make glass. After a few experiments, not, however, attended with very flattering prospects of success, he had the good fortune (or rather misfortune) by his persuasive and flattering tongue to inspire many of

---

* This hearse is the same that we now use; viz., 1832.

his neighbors and friends with a belief in the soundness of his theories, and the certain prospects of success that awaited them provided they would embark in the undertaking, and assist him to erect suitable buildings, procure workmen, and provide materials. Numbers of the solid and persevering cultivators of the soil, captivated by his Utopian schemes, were induced to lay aside the plough, the axe, and the spade, and mortgage their possessions, and lend their names and their influence to the proposed undertaking.

After considerable delay and many perplexing occurrences, they succeeded in completing the buildings of the manufactory and dwellings for the workmen ; and, having cast sand and salt and potash into the fire, *it came out glass.*

New adventurers were added to the list ; and considerable assistance was received from abroad : men of wealth and ambition were induced to come in and share in the prospective dividends that so surely awaited them.

They finally succeeded in making excellent cylinder glass ; * and were incorporated by the General Court, under the name of the Franklin Glass-Manufacturing Company, in Warwick. They did considerable business for a while, having obtained the confidence of the public generally. But a scarcity of money prevailing in the community tested the solvency of their capital: the banks refused to discount for a while ; and this proved a death-blow to all their operations. The fact was, that the business had been

---

* The first melting of glass blown here was on Sunday, Sept. 5, 1813.

got up and commenced without funds, or any knowledge or experience in the art of manufacturing glass: they had procured a foreigner (a Scotchman) of considerable ability, but of questionable integrity, to superintend their business, both in erecting the buildings, and superintending the workmen. They paid him extravagant wages; and, what was worse than that, they were subjected to his complete control, not having the ability or power to calculate for themselves, for want of knowledge in the art: they were consequently compelled to submit to his directions, and follow his ludicrous whims, however expensive, throughout all their various operations, to the no small detriment of their business and their purse. Workmen were also procured, and very high wages paid to them, and to those that understood blowing glass: months passed away before they were wanted; and large bounties in addition to all this were paid them to buy them off from their former employers, under the false pretext that it would be impossible to procure that particular kind of artisans unless the utmost secrecy was observed, and a liberal bonus offered as a temptation to induce them to leave other factories, and remove their families to this new and untried scene of operation.

The transactions of the Company had been carried on hitherto with too little attention to economy, which is so needful and necessary in all such establishments, especially in their infancy; and it could not withstand, all circumstances combined, the financial shock; and it sank to rise no more. Thus ended the speculations of the time: thus died the hopes of its friends ; and thus were blighted the quixotic visions of its deluded projector. But the void that remained after their dissolution was not so easily to be filled up — in particular, the ruined fortunes of many of the industrious inhabitants of this town, which must require years of untiring industry to amend and retrieve.

In December, 1813, the town voted their consent that the Universalist society in said town should be incorporated, with all the privileges and immunities granted to other religious societies.

1814.

This year the present pound was built : it was put up at auction, and struck off to Mr. Elliot Rawson for thirty-eight dollars.

In June the town voted unanimously to concur with the church in giving the Rev. Preserved Smith, jun., a call to settle in the gospel ministry in the town of Warwick; and a committee of nine persons was chosen to inform Mr. Smith of the proceedings of the town ; viz., Caleb Mayo, Ebenezer Pierce, Samuel Ball, Dr. Medad Pomeroy, Jonathan Blake, Justus Russell, William Cobb, Elijah Fisk, and Perley Leland. The town voted to grant Mr. Smith five hundred dollars annually for an encouragement to him to settle with us in the gospel ministry, and to pay him the first year's salary quarterly.

Sept. 5, it was voted to accept Mr. Smith's answer reported by the committee as follows, viz. : —

To the Church and Society in the Town of Warwick.

MY CHRISTIAN FRIENDS, — Having received by your committee an invitation to settle among you in the gospel ministry, I have endeavored to bestow all that attention to the subject which its importance demands. If I rightly understand the purport of the call you have been pleased to give me, I am to receive my stipend annually, so long as I continue your pastor.

Laying the above construction upon the subject, I do now, after having earnestly supplicated wisdom from the true source of all perfection to direct me in this decision, present you with this notice of my compliance with your request. In this procedure I have been influenced by the unanimous voice which so far prevailed in your exertions to re-establish a stated ministry, and in your proceedings towards electing me to that sacred office. And, in thus complying with your request, I trust I have studied duty and those things that may promote our mutual peace and happiness. It is not without fear and diffidence that I accept the important trust which you have judged expedient to devolve upon me: with diffidence, lest I do not possess those endowments which are of so high importance in constituting a faithful and successful minister of Christ; with fear, lest I should not discharge my functions to the glory of God, and to the saving of your souls. I therefore ask your Christian candor that you would look on me as composed of the same perishable materials as yourselves; that you accept my services, how imperfect soever they may seem in your opinion, as being the result of sincere intentions. For I feel the force of the apostle's exclamation, "Who is sufficient for these things?" Who is equal to this arduous work? And, while I bear your eternal interests in my remembrance at the throne of grace, I earnestly entreat you to commend me in your prayers to the great Head of the Church, that the divine grace, which alone is profitable to instruct and direct, may be my guide; that, when I have proclaimed the glorious prize of immortality to others, I shall not at last be rejected, as unfit for it, myself. Notwithstanding the gospel treasure of unspeakable value has been committed to *earthen vessels*, yet the power that accompanies its promulgation is derived from God. It is, therefore, incumbent upon us, as fellow-soldiers in the Christian warfare, to offer our united prayers to Deity, that his blessings may attend the ministration of his word, that not only our immortal interests may be promoted, but the glory of his moral government advanced, and the great laws of it more generally obeyed; that all who hear the voice of Christ may acknowledge *him as the only Bishop of their souls*, as in the Redeemer's kingdom there shall be only one fold and one Shepherd.

Bearing such reflections in mind, let us ever adhere with firm and inflexible steadiness to our Christian profession, and aim at making continual improvement in it, from a full persuasion that our labors in love, and attention to Christianity, will finally be accompanied with a glorious reward.

PRESERVED SMITH, JR.

It was proposed in town-meeting to choose a committee of five, to transact the business of the ordination; and chose William Cobb, Ashbel Ward, William Burnett, jun., Perez Allen, and Justus Russell; and it was voted that the expense of the ordination be drawn out of the ministry money then in the treasury. Accordingly the Rev. Preserved Smith, jun., was ordained as pastor over the First Congregational Church and Society in Warwick, on Oct. 12, 1814.

In April, 1815, a report of a committee on the petition of Caleb Mayo, Esq., in favor of Widow

Abigail Reed, was reported to the town, and accepted, which was as follows ; viz. : —

We, the subscribers, being appointed a committee at the annual meeting in March last to take into consideration the request of Caleb Mayo, Esq., for, and in behalf of, the widow of the late Rev. Samuel Reed, have attended to the business of our appointment, and report as follows : —

That, in examining the former records, Mr. Reed was settled in the gospel ministry in this town in 1779, and was to receive his stipend in proportion to rye at three shillings and sixpence, and corn at two shillings and ninepence, per bushel, and pork at threepence half-penny per pound, from an incorporated society; and that he continued to receive his salary in full for fifteen years. We find, by contract entered into the third of March, 1794, Mr. Reed did become the town's minister, and after that to receive his salary in silver and gold; and we do not find by any of the records that he received any thing different from his stated salary for ten years from that date ; and in further examination we find that from 1804 to 1811, which is eight years, Mr. Reed received $312.75 more than his stated salary. We learn that when Mr. Reed became the town's minister he received a certain sum of the town's money, and secured the town by mortgage of his real estate. We learn by Mrs. Reed's signing the mortgage she is debarred of any dowry in his real estate. We also learn that by the aid of Mrs. Reed's friends, before the judge of probate, she is to receive $200.00 out of Mr. Reed's estate for her own use and disposal. We also learn, that, since Mr. Reed's decease, Mrs. Reed, by the aid of her friends, has had the good fortune to get upon the list of the Massachusetts Congregational Charitable Society for the relief of destitute widows and children of deceased ministers, and has for two years past received about thirty dollars per year, and will probably continue to receive her proportion of the money in the funds of said society. After learning all these facts, we, your committee, are unanimously of opinion that it will be more for the harmony of the citizens of this town to have the business indefinitely postponed than to take any further measures upon it.

All which is submitted by your committee.

JUSTUS RUSSELL,
PEREZ ALLEN, } *Committee.*
JOSEPH DRAPER,

In April, 1817, the town voted to accept the following report; viz.: —

The subscribers, having been appointed a committee, at the annual meeting in March last, to take into consideration the fifteenth article in the warrant of said meeting, relative to the ministry and school funds in the town of Warwick, report their opinion, viz.: That eight dollars and seventy-six cents of the interest of the unapplied ministry-money now in the treasury be added to the ministry-fund, in order to increase the fund to nine hundred dollars. And that the sum of one dollar of the overlays of the town-tax the present year be added to the school-fund in order to increase that fund to five hundred dollars; and that all the loans of said funds now existing, excepting what is secured by mortgage of real estate, shall, on or before the first day of January next, be collected, and paid into the treasury, or be secured by mortgage of real estate; and that the said funds, after that date, should be loaned by the selectmen of the town to the inhabitants of the town of Warwick, in sums not less than one hundred dollars, nor over two hundred dollars, to be secured by mortgage of real estate to double the amount, to be appraised by the selectmen of said town; and the person or persons that shall not pay the interest to the treasurer on or before the first day of January, annually, shall not be entitled to the continuance of said loan; and that no person shall have a loan a longer time than three years at a time, on condition that others want it for equally good security.

JOSHUA ATWOOD,
JUSTUS RUSSELL, } <i>Committee.</i>
ASHBEL WARD,

At an adjournment of this meeting, it was voted to reconsider a part of the report of the committee respecting the ministry and school funds, so as to extend the time of payment to ten years, upon the condition of paying ten per cent of the principal annually, and the interest on such sums as may be loaned to the inhabitants of said town.

At the adjournment in May it was voted to build a powder-magazine for the security of the town-stores, as follows, viz.: Eight feet square, to be built of good, well-burnt bricks laid in lime mortar, the walls to be seven feet high, with a square roof, well boarded and shingled, and to be ceiled with good white pine boards planed on the inside, and a good, double floor well nailed; the door to be double, with a good lock and key; the walls to be eight inches thick; and a foundation of flat stones to be built in a workmanlike manner. A committee of three was chosen to superintend the building of said magazine; viz., Amos K. Whitney, Caleb Mayo, William Cobb.

1818.

April 4, 1818, voted to accept the report of the committee respecting the purchase of the burying-ground as follows: —

The subscribers, having been chosen a committee to complete the purchase of land of Mr. Bunyan Penniman for an addition to the burying-ground, have attended that service, and report as follows: That we have obtained a deed of said Penniman of one acre and fifty rods of land, measuring fifteen rods on the road, fifteen rods on the south line, twelve rods on the west line, and fifteen rods and thirteen links on the north line, and have paid him sixty-five dollars and sixty-two cents as a consideration for the same, it being understood that the town is to fence said land.

CALEB MAYO, } *Committee.*
WILLIAM COBB,

It was voted that the same committee that purchased the ground to make an addition to the burying-ground be a committee to fence the same.

It was wisely said by the wise king of Israel that "*there is a time for every thing;*" and purchasing this spot of ground to enlarge our burying-place was one of those transactions that was performed in its proper time. A more judicious and timely act is not to be found on our public records.

1820.

In August, 1820, a meeting of the inhabitants of the town was convened, on the question whether it was expedient that delegates should be chosen to meet in convention to amend the Constitution of this Commonwealth. On sorting and counting the votes, it appeared that there were thirty-two votes against it, and forty-three in favor of the measure.

In October, Jonathan Blake, jun., was chosen a delegate to attend the aforesaid convention.

1821.

In April, 1821, the articles of amendment proposed by the convention for altering the constitution of the State were laid before the town for their approval or rejection; and but two out of the fourteen articles were accepted; viz., the eighth and fourteenth. The amendments were not popular in this town.

A brief account of the *tornado* that passed over the south part of Warwick, an occurrence that may well be remembered by many of the sufferers, but which, for the information of posterity, ought to be preserved, as a very frightful, destructive, and uncommon occurrence: —

On the ninth day of September, 1821, a tremendous whirlwind passed over the south part of this town, most appalling and terrific in its appearance, and most destructive in its consequences. I was an eye-witness of this most sublime and astonishing phenomenon of Nature; and language is too feeble to express my feelings, or to properly and accurately describe the majestic and interesting scene.

It was on the day instituted by our benevolent Creator for a day of rest that this awful calamity befell us, when, if ever (after the solemn services of the sanctuary are ended), the minds of rational and intelligent beings are composed and calm, and the benign and beneficial influences of religion pervade the heart. Just as the sun was sinking behind the western hills, an appearance of agitation or concussion was discovered in the clouds: slight showers of rain had fallen in several places in this vicinity during the afternoon, and the heat had been oppressive. The commotion in the clouds had something of the appearance of the angry billows of the ocean when raging at the utmost extent of their fury. These agitations and concussions soon blended together, and assumed a form, which at first sight resembled a column of smoke ascending from the conflagration of a building, or the burning of pine timber on new lands; but it soon became more compactly embodied and more visible, and moved along with a majesty and grandeur inexpressibly surprising, powerful, and great. Its appearance was in the shape of an inverted cone: the bottom, like the besom of destruction, swept every thing before it; and the top besieged the heavens. The embodied appearance of this elemental strife was black, dense, solid, and compact; and it sustained its form with all the regularity of a magnificent temple. It moved almost direct from the west towards the east: detached pieces of buildings, such as timber, boards, shingles, limbs of trees, leaves, grass, and, in short, fragments of every kind, were thrown out of its vortex in every direction, filling and darkening the air. Birds, especially hawks and crows, were sailing round and round, high in the air aloof from the storm, expressing their dismay by dismal screams. But above all the tremendous crashing, stunning, deafening noise, not unlike heavy thunder or the internal bellowings of an earthquake, which caused the earth to tremble under us, and seemed to forebode its final dissolution, it filled us with sensations too sublime and too awful to be adequately expressed. Thus far I have described the visible appearance and movement of this scene of terror and destruction ; and now I will attempt to give a short and imperfect account of its effects.

Its first appearance in the clouds was discovered to be not far from Connecticut River. It was high up from the water, and did not begin its work of destruction until it came in contact with the earth, near the top of the high ridge of land called Northfield Mountains. The first building it destroyed was Mr. Garland's house ; the next were Chapin Holden's house and barn : these buildings were in Northfield. Mr. Joseph Willson's house and barn in Warwick were entirely torn from their foundations, and some of his family badly injured. Mr. Elisha Brown's house was also destroyed ; and one of his daughters, about thirteen years of age, buried in the ruins, and killed : another daughter was permanently injured. These were in Warwick. In the north-westerly part of Orange, Capt. Moses Smith's tavern-house, with barns and sheds, were all swept away in a moment. In the twinkling of an eye they were scattered in every direction ; and a young woman by the name of Stearns, about eighteen years of age, in the bloom of youth (an inmate of the house), was thus instantly called to her final account. Only the two persons above mentioned perished; but many were severely wounded. Some cattle were killed, and others much injured. Five dwelling-houses and thirteen barns were either entirely destroyed or unroofed; and many more sustained some damage.

It is impossible to describe this scene of destruction the morning after the calamity. The resistless fury of the wind had laid low the dwellings and other buildings of many of our townsmen and friends. Woodland, orchards, stone walls, and even large rocks, were no impediment to its force.* The wake of the whirlwind was literally covered with wood, timber, boards, shingles, hay, straw, and fragments of every thing conceivable. Heavy logs that had lain years on the ground, and were embedded considerably in the soil, were torn out of their resting-places, and in many instances were broken to pieces. Several rocks that would weigh a ton or more were started from their beds, and moved a considerable distance. Household furniture and clothing were strewed over the ground, rent and torn, and dashed to pieces. Many articles of value were found in other towns east of us, and a few of them were not materially injured. A part of the roof of a building was found twenty-five miles from the place whence it was taken; and a part of a leaf of an account-book was found in Groton, about sixty miles from the house where it was deposited in a chamber. The next day after this awful visitation the town assembled, and chose a committee to ascertain the loss of the inhabitants, and agreed to

---

* See Appendix, page 188.

raise four hundred dollars, to be distributed among the sufferers in proportion to each one's loss, or as nearly so as the committee should think proper.

1822.

In 1822 a committee was chosen to report the best method to be pursued by the town in choosing, organizing, and empowering our school committee in future.

The report of this committee contains sentiments honorable and laudable in themselves, and of great importance to the town; and it is a matter of regret that we have so soon forgotten such salutary advice.

Here follows the report, viz.:—

The subscribers having been chosen a committee to report a plan for the better regulation and examination of the schools in the town of Warwick,— impressed with the opinion that the subject of the education of youth, as it respects science and morals, which are by law required to be taught in our common schools, is of the highest importance to society; that there cannot be too much attention and patronage given to this subject by the public; that a well-regulated and uniform system of instruction throughout the several school-districts in the town would be of great advantage to the community,— to effect the above the following is respectfully submitted:—

1st. That it is expedient to choose a committee annually: that this committee consist of two persons, whose duty it shall be (together with the minister of the town) to visit and inspect the several schools twice in a season; viz., near the commencement, and before the close, of the winter term.

2d. As strangers and foreigners from different parts of the country are frequently intrusted with the charge of instructing our children, therefore that this committee be authorized to recommend and introduce such modes of instruction, and such books, as, in their judgment, are best adapted to promote the great object for which our schools were established.

3d. That any person presuming to take the charge of any school within the limits of the town, as an instructor, shall be required to produce to the committee of the district who contracts with him, and to the examining committee on their first examination, such credentials as the law requires.

4th. That as large sums of money have been frequently paid to those whose services as instructors have been injurious, rather than beneficial, to our youth, that this committee, noting any such defect on their first examination, shall report the same to the district in which he may be engaged.

5th. That this committee (the minister excepted) receive from the town a reasonable compensation for their services if performed agreeable to the foregoing report.

AMOS TAYLOR,
LEMUEL WHEELOCK,
JOSEPH STEVENS,   } Committee.
JOSIAH PROCTOR,
JAMES GOLDSBURY,

The town voted to accept of this report, and chose a committee of two persons, agreeable to its recommendation; but how soon have they forgotten or disregarded these useful hints!

In 1823 the present hearse-house was built, under the superintendence of Abijah Eddy, Isaac Hastings, jun., and William Cobb, — a committee chosen by the town for that purpose.

1824.

In 1824 the meeting-house was painted, and the windows and plastering repaired.

1832.

On the 23d of April, 1832, a number of the inhabitants of Warwick turned out voluntarily, and procured and set out about sixty rock-maple trees around the burying-ground, and a spruce-tree in the centre, and one each side of the south gate.

Thus, in an imperfect manner, I have detailed to you the origin of many of the principal events that have transpired in this place since civilized man has claimed dominion over it; and, in closing, perhaps a few observations on the situation of the town, the productions of the soil, manners of the inhabitants, longevity, &c., will not be misplaced.

Warwick is situated in the north-east corner of Franklin County, seventy-seven and a half miles from Boston by the stage-road, and twenty miles from Greenfield (the shire-town of the county), having the State of New Hampshire on the north, and joining Winchester and Richmond in that State; on the east by Royalston in the County of Worcester, and Orange in the County of Franklin; south on an unincorporated tract of land called Erving's Grant; west on said grant, and the town of Northfield. It contained originally twenty-three thousand acres of land before the south-east corner of it was set off to Orange. The surface is broken and hilly, and a high hill called Mount Grace occupies a very prominent station near the centre of the town. In many places the soil is so rocky and broken as to render it unfit for cultivation : in other places, tolerably good ; not so suitable for English grain as for grass, corn, and potatoes. The principal exports are beef, cattle, butter, and cheese; but not so much of these as formerly. Braiding straw and palm-leaf hats is the principal occupation of the women, excepting attending to the dairy and other household affairs. The inhabitants, generally speaking, are hardy, industrious, and persevering, principally cultivators of the earth ; sober, intelligent, and of steady habits, averse to idleness, and aloof from extreme poverty : perhaps as much on an equality as any town in the Commonwealth, — none extravagantly rich, and none miserably poor. The climate is healthy and the air salubrious, and the water is not surpassed by any on earth. The principal disease is consumption ; not exempt, however, from fevers, and the numberless little petty diseases incident to man. Only one person has ever died in this town that was over one hundred years of age ; and that was a Mrs. Willson, who was about one hundred and two years old when she died. As a proof of the longevity of its inhabitants, in a population of eleven hundred and fifty, there are now living forty-six individuals over seventy years of age, — twenty-three men and twenty-three women. Twenty-five of them are over eighty years, — thirteen men and twelve women ; three over ninety years, — two men and one woman ; the oldest man ninety-three years, the oldest woman ninety-one years. The aggregate ages of the thirteen men that exceed eighty years is eleven hundred and four years ; and of the twelve women, ten hundred and ninety-seven years : total aggregate amount of the twenty-five oldest persons is two thousand two hundred and one years. It is presumed this falls years short of the exact truth, as there are no fractions counted, although some of them amount to almost a year.

There is now the Congregational society in this town, Rev. Preserved Smith, pastor, which comprises about one half of the voters and taxable property ; a Universalist incorporated society ; part of a Baptist society, incorporated with a part of Royalston, Elder Marshal, minister ; part of another Baptist society, who are connected with some of the inhabitants of Erving's Grant and New Salem, Elder John Shepardson, teacher ; and a few Methodists who belong to a Methodist society in Northfield, and have a meeting-house in the South Woods (so called). Here follows a list of the names of all the persons that have ever been chosen and served as town-officers, with the number of years they served, when known.* There have been two settled ministers of the Congregational order before the present one, Rev. Preserved Smith ; viz., Rev. Lemuel Hedge and Rev. Samuel Reed.

Rev. Lemuel Hedge was ordained, and a church

* See Appendix, page 192.

gathered, Dec. 3, 1760. Rev. Mr. Forbes of Brookfield preached the sermon from 1st Timothy, 4th chap., 6th verse. Ministers present, — Mr. Forbes, Mr. Hubbard of Northfield. Mr. Frink of Rutland District was moderator, and gave the charge. The covenant was signed by Lemuel Hedge, David Ayres, Ebenezer Davis, Ephraim Perry, David Burnett, John Farrar, Asa Robbins, Charles Woods, James Ball, Jeduthan Morse, Amzi Doolittle, and Silas Town. Rev. Lemuel Hedge died Oct. 17, 1777, in the forty-seventh year of his age, and the seventeenth of his ministry. The sermon at his funeral was preached by the Rev. Bunker Gay of Hinsdale, N.H. Rev. Samuel Reed was ordained Sept. 23, 1779, and died July 31, 1812. Rev. Joseph Lee of Royalston preached the sermon at his funeral. There was a great congregation present. Rev. Preserved Smith, jun., was ordained Oct. 12, 1814, and still remains here (viz., 1832). There has been one Universalist minister, the Rev. Caleb Rich, and two Baptist ministers, the Rev. Levi Hodge, and Rev. John Shepardson, that have resided in town previous to the above date.

———

Almost one generation has passed away since I commenced and wrote the first part of the history of Warwick. The first settlers have all passed off the stage of action; and most of the then aged and worthy members of society have followed them to their final resting-place, — the grave. Those then in the prime of manhood are either dead, or tottering in old age; those that were young then are bearing the public burdens, and filling the ranks made thin by the great Destroyer; and those unborn at that time have arrived to adult age, and are busily employed on the great theatre of life. The grand object of the historian ought to be a desire to perpetuate the truth, to transmit to all coming time a fair record of all the passing events, uninfluenced by present party-feelings, and above all disguise and hypocritical cant.

Now (in 1854) a blank of twenty-two years is to be filled; and I shall begin where I left off in 1832.

1833.

In 1833 some proposed amendments to the constitution of the State were laid before the town for their approval or rejection; and there were one hundred and eighteen yeas to nine nays.

1834.

In 1834 the school-fund was separated from the ministerial fund; and the town voted that it should be loaned on land security: it amounted to five hundred dollars.

This year the town built a new pound; and also the school-districts were defined anew by a committee chosen for that purpose, consisting of Jonathan Blake, jun., Josiah Proctor, and Lemuel Wheelock.

1836.

In 1836 the first religious society in Warwick (Unitarian) built a new meeting-house, which is now standing (in 1854), being the third house built for, or by, that society. It stands a little west of where the two others stood, and on the west side of the county-road. It is not large, but a neat, well-proportioned edifice, erected by subscription of the members of the parish, at a cost of about three thousand dollars. The house contains sixty slips, or pews, which will seat five grown persons each: no gallery except in front, expressly for the singers. It has a fine-toned bell, weighing a thousand and eighty-nine pounds, which cost three hundred and fifty dollars, which is included in the first-mentioned sum. This was the first church-bell that was ever purchased in Warwick. The above bell was warranted for one year; and before the year was out it broke, and was returned to Boston and exchanged for another which was a few pounds lighter, without any cost to the society except the freight each way, and the trouble attending. This bell was also warranted for one year, and lasted until early in 1841, when it gave out also. The society then thought it best to try at Ames's foundry in Springfield, carried the old bell there, and exchanged for a new one, of about the same weight, and paid the difference between old metal and new: this bell remains sound to this day; viz., 1865.

The house has a well-finished vestry in the basement, for the use of the sabbath school, public meetings, &c. The subscribers chose Jonathan Blake, jun., Joseph Stevens, and Samuel Moore, a committee, to contract for building the house, and superintending its erection. It was raised the eighth day of September,

1836. The hands that raised the meeting-house took dinner at Asa Taft's Hotel with the architect and contractor, Mr. Chapin Holden, two ministers, two doctors, two deacons, and the building-committee by invitation, numbering in all seventy-four. The pews were appraised by a committee, and then put up at auction for a choice, and all sold, bringing four hundred and seven dollars more than the cost of the house, which was expended in furniture for the house, and in finishing the vestry.*

There was an Orthodox society formed in 1829, in this town, partly from seceders from the first society (Unitarian), and a few others, and organized a church, consisting of thirty members; and in 1833 they built a meeting-house, at a cost of about thirteen hundred dollars. This house stands on the land formerly occupied by the Franklin Glass-Factory Company, and near where their main buildings were located, and is a short distance south of the town's common and the Unitarian meeting-house. On the sixth day of November, 1833, the Rev. Samuel Kingsbury was settled as their pastor. He preached for them about two years, and was then dismissed. The Rev. Roger C. Hatch was ordained as their second pastor on the twenty-third day of December, 1835, and was dismissed June 22, 1853.

In 1840, at the April meeting, an article of amendment to the constitution of the State was voted on; and there were eighty-three yeas, and fourteen nays.

In 1850 the school-districts were regularly and

* See Plan.

contr
doct
invit
were
aucti
dred
hous
and
Th
this
(Un
con
a m
doll
pied
nea
a sh
Uni
ber,
their
and
was
thir
22,
I
me
and
nay
I

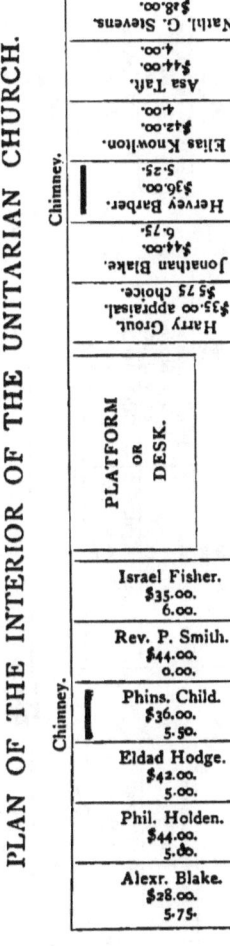

PLAN OF THE INTERIOR OF THE UNITARIAN CHURCH.

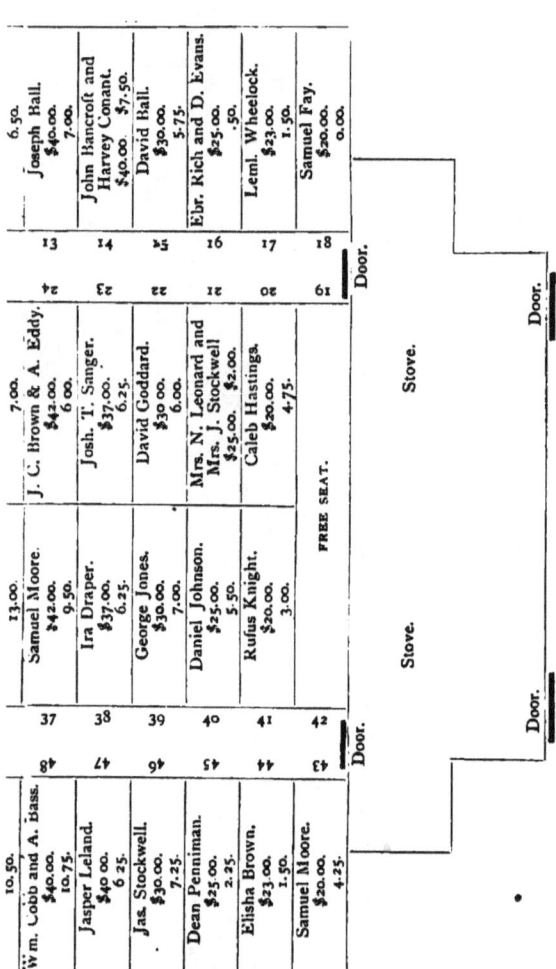

Interior arrangement of the Unitarian Meeting-House in Warwick. Raised Sept. 8, 1836. Dedicated Jan. 18, 1837. As you enter, in the spaceway are two stoves; the funnels pass into the house over the doors, and enter the chimneys at the opposite end of the house. Also two flights of stairs to the singers' gallery. Inside, the platform or desk is just as high as the tops of the pews: a sofa for a seat, and a table with a curtain, stands on the front of it. The figures in the aisles are the numbers of the slips. The upper figures in the slips are the appraisal ; the lower figures, the sum given for choice. The two sums are the cost of each slip. The appraisal covers the whole cost of the house ($2,526.00), except the bell and some few donations. With the choice-money, which is $407.00, we purchased furniture for the house, such as chandelier, carpets, &c.
S. B.

lawfully bounded by the selectmen by proper metes and bounds; and a high stone monument with stones about it, and the number of the district on its face at each angle and corner; and the eleventh district altered to ten; and districts No. 3 and No. 9 were united; and ten permanent districts formed, and accepted by the town.

A dispute about the line between Widow Rhoda Wheelock's thirds and the town-common was this year settled by a reference composed of Richard Colton of Northfield, Ozias Roberts of Gill, and Jered Weed of Petersham.

They were chosen mutually by the selectmen and the said Widow Wheelock; and their award was accepted by the parties, and the north-east corner of the common permanently established.

In 1851 the legal voters of the town were called upon to give in their votes in favor of, or against, calling a convention to amend and revise the State constitution: yeas, 113; nays, 71.

In 1852 they were again called to vote on the same question, when a hundred and twenty-eight voted in favor of calling a convention, and sixty-nine against it.

In 1853 they chose Samuel W. Spooner a delegate to the convention to be convened at Boston to make amendments to the constitution of the State.

At the November meeting following they were called upon to accept or refuse the adoption of the new constitution as amended, and to be laid before the people: and the votes were, for adopting the same, a hundred and seven votes; opposed to it, sixty-six votes.

The money voted to be raised by the town this year, 1853, viz., is as follows:—

For the support of poor, and other contingent
    expenses $1,500.00
For repairing highways 800.00
For schools 700.00
                        Total . . $3,000.00

School-money received from the State . . $48.95
Interest of the Town School-Fund . . . 30.00
Total expended for schooling this year . . 778.95

Amount of town debts $1,338.00

Number of ratable polls in town, two hundred and forty-four.

There are now four religious societies in Warwick; viz., one Unitarian, one Orthodox, one Baptist, one Universalist, and a few Methodists that belong to a society in Northfield.

The Universalist society was incorporated in February, 1814: they have no meeting-house. The other three societies have each of them one, situated in or near the middle of the town.

There is no settled minister of any denomination in the town at the present time, There is but one doctor, Amos Taylor, who came here in 1815 or 1816.

There is no. lawyer: never had but one, Henry Barnard, Esq. Not many very important or interesting events have transpired in the past twenty-two years.

Public and private affairs have moved on in the current of time, with their usual progressive, but not very exciting, fluctuations. Party spirit has been kept alive, and has marked out its alternate rise and fall of the contending parties.

For the largest share of the time the Democratic party has been in the ascendency, and carried a majority of the votes. At this time the Whig and Democratic parties are nearly balanced; and the Free-soil party numbers nearly one-fifth of the votes.

The town has gradually decreased in the number of its inhabitants for thirty years past, as will be seen by the census.

The farms, as a general thing, are not so productive as they were forty years ago. Many pieces of tillage-land are nearly worn out (as we term it). Peach-trees are a complete failure; and not one-tenth part so many apples are now raised as at that time. The trees have become old and decayed, and but few young ones are set out to replace them, although some attention has been paid to grafting of late. The pasture-lands, which were formerly good, have greatly deteriorated, and are almost covered with noxious bushes, brakes, and ferns; and they yield comparatively little to their former products. The hay is also reduced in quantity as well as quality. Less rye and wheat is raised than formerly, but quite as much Indian corn; oats less, and barley probably more. The greatest manufacturing interest in the town is its lumber. Large quantities of white-pine timber have been manufactured here in times past: the old growth is becoming scarce, being nearly all cut off. Considerable quantities of the second growth of pines are now sawed into pail-staves, and other articles of various kinds. The hard wood is worked into chair-stuff, brush-woods, and broom-handles.

There are fifteen saw-mills in the town, which annually send to market more than one million feet of lumber. There are three pail-stave shops, and three or four shops with circular saws attached, to cut chair-plank and many other small articles; one axe-shop, three blacksmith-shops, and three tanneries; three stores (one of them is a small union-store), one tavern, and one post-office. The decline of population and of business in this town may be mainly attributed to its exclusion from the privilege of a railroad passing through it; while all the adjoining towns but one have a railroad dépôt to accommodate them, and facilitate the transportation of their productions to market.

Although I know little of geology, I am induced to believe, from the few discoveries that have been made by scientific men, and the many indications so apparent on its surface, of mineral productions, that Warwick will one day be rich in her inexhaustible stores of iron and lead and copperas and firestone, and many other valuable and useful articles in manufactures and commerce.

· Little, however, has been discovered yet; but that little may authorize us to expect an abundant supply of many of the foregoing articles, and others, perhaps, not now thought of.

I will state, from memory and traditionary lore, some facts and discoveries which I myself have seen, or heard from others. As to iron-ore, that is abundant in many places within the town, I know very well.

As to the extent of the bog-ore I cannot say; but I can say, that, within my memory, the sound of the trip-hammer was regularly heard from day to day, and iron of the best quality was there manufactured. I have now a small piece of chain which was made from that ore : it is strong, tough, and very malleable. For many years it was used with a draught-chain on the ground to draw logs and timber ; and seldom would a link break in that chain, although not more than half the size of the other.

For want of proper encouragement, or want of funds, or for some other cause to me unknown, the business was stopped. I have heard it stated that the ore failed ; and well it might, as but one little spot was ever opened or searched out to my knowledge ; and millions of tons may now lie concealed above and below that place, and may forever lie so concealed, unless some accidental discovery, or some scientific research, is made to bring it to light. The old forge stood about two miles southerly from the centre of the town, and a little below *Morse's Pond*, near where Dea. George W. Moore's saw-mill now is.

About one mile south of this place is *Round Mountain* (so called) : on its north-easterly side there are many striking indications of iron and copperas, the stones slacking when exposed to the light and air, and emitting a sulphurous smell. A little more than a mile south of this place, as I was surveying a piece of land forty years ago, my attention was called by the proprietor of the land to a certain spot where he had dug a hole about a foot or a foot and a half deep, as he said, to find the brimstone ; and it smelled very strong of that article. It was of a red or yellowish color. I took a little, and rubbed it in my hands: it not only colored them, but the smell of brimstone continued even after I had washed them thoroughly.

I intended, when Prof. Hitchcock made the geological survey of the State, to have been present, and shown him, not only *this*, but several other places and substances that I could have pointed out to him within the limits of the town; one in particular, where a certain kind of earth, or paint, is found, which, as tradition tells the story, a man living near by used to dig, and use to paint his cart-wheels.

The owner of the land, who is now dead, told me that he called it his *terre de Seine*, as it resembled the earth which is found on the banks of the River *Seine* in France, from which it derived its name. Black-lead is also found in this town, many rocks being found that have black-lead in their interstices. Iron-ore has been found on Mount Grace; and also pure lead was found on its north-east lobe (*Bennett's Knob*) by one of the first settlers: he had the iron-ore experimented on, which resulted in the fact that it was too unmalleable and too brittle for common wrought-iron.

There is iron-rock ore on the Daniel Johnson Farm, in the east part of Warwick, near the old turnpike-road that leads to Orange. Many years ago, there were considerable quantities of it dug, and carted to Worcester to be made into emery.

There is also firestone, or freestone, discovered by Prof. Hitchcock when he surveyed the State, and believed to be inexhaustible, situated only about half a mile from the middle of the town. For a proper description of the two last-mentioned articles, reference may be had to said Hitchcock's Geological Report, in every town-clerk's office in the State.

There is a place on the farm, formerly owned by Mr. Wilder Stevens, where there are several *Indian mortars*, as they are called ; viz., deep and nearly round, smooth holes in the solid rock, and three or four feet deep ; and the largest is perhaps two feet across : they are as smooth as if worn out by water, and similar to some holes that I have seen in the bed of Deerfield River, in a dry time at Shelburne Falls ; and what renders it more remarkable is the fact that they are located on the highest land (excepting the mountain-tops) between the valley of Miller's River on the south and the Ashuelot on the north, near where the water descends each way towards those rivers.

On land formerly owned by Mr. Nathan Hastings, there is a place, under a shelving rock, that was once a bear's den ; and a young cub was caught there, and Mrs. Hastings actually nursed it at her own breast. Not a great distance from that place, on Mr. Thomas Mallard's farm, there is a hole in the ledges, where formerly, if a stone was dropped into it, the stone might be heard to rattle down, down, until out of hearing. Subsequently the boys have thrown in so many stones, that the passage has got stopped up ; and the stones do not now descend far into the cavern.

Mount Grace is situated near the centre of Warwick, and is one of the highest mountains in the State (according to State survey, it is sixteen hundred and twenty-eight feet high). The water runs out of this town, east, west, north, and south. To the east and south it falls into Miller's River; to the north into the Ashuelot at Winchester, N.H.; and west into the Connecticut River in Northfield.

In the year 1830 I surveyed and measured all the roads in Warwick, and made a plan of the town, for a map of the State. There were seventy-six miles of county and town roads at that time; and there must be about the same now. There have been quite a number of roads laid out and built at great expense since that time, and many have been discontinued.

Among the early settlers of this town, we find the names of Joseph Goodell, Samuel Bennet, Dea. James Ball, Amos Marsh, Solomon Eager, Thomas Rich, Moses Leonard, Col. Samuel Williams, Dea. Silas Towne, Col. Joseph Mayo, Caleb Mayo, Capt. John Goldsbury, Capt. Mark Moore, and Jonathan Moore. Some of the above have descendants still living here; and others we know nothing of, except from the records.

In the winter of 1832 there were forty-six individuals in the town that were over seventy years of age; twenty-three men, and twenty-three women. I now find, on Feb. 1, 1854, the following list of aged people;* but not one of them was seventy years old when I then wrote: those forty-six have all died, or removed from town, within twenty-two years.

See Appendix, page 198.

CONTINUATION

OF THE HISTORY OF WARWICK FROM 1854 TO 1872, BY
DEACON HERVEY BARBER.

August, 1854. — The town voted to instruct the town-agent (James Stockwell) to ascertain whether a new trial on the Murdock case can be had; also voted to pay the expense of transporting the baggage of the Warwick Light Infantry to and from the place of encampment the present year.

May, 1855. — The town voted upon the several amendments to the Constitution of the Commonwealth, passed by the last two legislatures, as follows: —

Art. 1, yeas 31, nays 3; Art. 2, yeas 34, nays 0; Art. 3, yeas 34, nays 0; Art. 4, yeas 34, nays 0; Art. 5, yeas 34, nays 0; Art. 6, yeas 34, nays 0.

March 17, 1856. — Article 4 in the warrant for a town-meeting is as follows: "To see if the town will vote to purchase or hire a farm for the purpose of supporting the town-paupers, or act thereon." Also voted that the selectmen be a committee to receive proposals for a town-farm, and report at an adjourned meeting.

Voted to adjourn this meeting until two weeks from this date, to hear said report.

At the adjourned meeting, the selectmen made the following report: —

Received proposals from Asa Bancroft for his home-
    farm, with the buildings thereon, at . . . $2,700
Of Dea. Sylvanus Ward for his home-farm and build-
    ings, at 2,000
For his Ashbell Ward place and buildings . . 1,000
From Daniel Felton for his home-farm and buildings, 1,700
From S. T. Delvee for his home-farm and buildings, 1,500

They also report, that, in their opinion, the town can save $300 per year by purchasing Dea. Ward's home-farm, or Asa Bancroft's; and recommend to the town to choose a committee to investigate the subject, and authorize said committee to purchase such farm as they may think proper.

                IBRI BAKER,
                CLARK STEARNS, } *Committee.*
                H. G. MALLARD,

WARWICK, March 31, 1856.

Voted to lay the report on the table: afterwards the town voted to purchase a town-farm.

Also voted to choose a committee of seven persons, including the selectmen, to purchase a farm on which to support the paupers of the town.

Voted and chose the selectmen by nomination.

Voted, and chose Edward Mayo, James Stockwell, S. N. Atwood, and Hervey Barber, by ballot. Said committee, after examining the farms in the above report, and Ezekiel Ellis's, Joseph W. Phillips's, and Kimball Whitney's, and conferring with the owners, and considerable consultation among themselves, voted, six to one, to purchase the Bancroft Farm. A few days after, said committee purchased of Asa

Bancroft his home-farm and a wood-lot adjoining for the sum of $2,700. They soon purchased stock, tools, and furniture sufficient for the use of said farm and house, for $1,300; and early in May following they hired a man and his wife to take charge of the establishment, under the superintendence of the selectmen, for the sum of $175.

Our town-farm has been improved, and nearly all of the paupers have been supported in that manner, from that time to the present (1872), to the satisfaction of a large majority of the inhabitants of the town. Our paupers have a comfortable home, without the continued suspense of removal from year to year, as was the previous custom, when their maintenance was contracted for by the year to those that were willing to take them the cheapest; and even under that form of support, for some years previous to maintaining an almshouse, it cost the town over six hundred dollars per annum: but, since we have adopted the present system, the largest expense per annum has been but a little over three hundred dollars, and some years less than one-half that amount; and one year the cost to the town was only twenty-four and a half cents per week for each person supported, including interest on money invested, labor, clothing for paupers, doctor's bills, and all other necessary expenses for the year,— the growth of stock and the products of farm paying all the other expenses. And we have supported from eight to twelve persons during all these years, all being old and feeble people, able to perform but very little labor,— a larger number than would be the average for as many years previous to the purchase of the town-farm.

Aug. 31, 1856. — Voted to give School District No. 1 leave to build a schoolhouse on the common, near where the old meeting-house stood. During the autumn, the present schoolhouse was built on the spot where it now stands.

May 1, 1857. — The inhabitants met and voted upon the following amendments to the Constitution of the Commonwealth, that were agreed upon by the legislatures of 1856 and 1857: Art. 1, 48 yeas, 34 nays; Art. 2, 36 yeas, 46 nays; Art. 3, 44 yeas, 38 nays. Also voted to raise $1,000 for the purpose of paying off the town-debt.

1858. — At a legal town-meeting, the town voted and chose Henry G. Mallard agent to take charge of the pauper case, commenced against the inhabitants of Warwick by the town of Northfield, with instructions to manage the case as he thinks will be for the best interests of the town. This case was prosecuted to final judgment; the result being that the pauper (Miss Adeline Phelps), an insane person, was assigned to the town of Northfield for her future support.

March 1. — Voted to notify all future town-meetings by posting an attested copy of the warrant at the post-office, and another at Scott's store, and a notice at each meeting-house in town, seven days previous to the meeting.

March 7, 1859. — Voted that a copy of the warrant be posted at the hotel, instead of Scott's store.

May 9, 1858. — The inhabitants of the town met at a legal town-meeting, and voted upon the amendment to the Constitution of the Commonwealth, agreed upon by its last two legislatures, as follows: Yeas, 6; nays, 36.

Oct. 2, 1858. — The funerals of Lemuel Scott and Henry G. Mallard were attended from the Unitarian church; a large audience being present, and in full sympathy with the afflicted families, as two young men in the midst of their usefulness were suddenly stricken down by typhoid-fever, causing a sadness not often experienced by the people of the town since its first settlement.

May 7, 1860. — The inhabitants of the town met at a legal town-meeting, and gave in their votes on the amendments of the Constitution agreed upon by the last two legislatures of the Commonwealth, as follows: Article 1, 18 yeas, 1 nay; Article 2, 8 yeas, 11 nays.

The whole number of persons between the ages of eighteen and forty-five enrolled in the militia, May, 1860, was 145.

March 2, 1861. — The whole amount of indebtedness of the town, as per report of selectmen, over and above resources, was $2,527.03.

Nov. 1. — The selectmen of the towns of Orange and Warwick met, according to appointment, and erected stone monuments on the town-line, beside each of the highways running between said towns, as provided by chapter 84 of the Acts of 1861; and the selectmen of Northfield and Warwick performed the same service on the line of their towns Nov. 13 of the same year; also the aforesaid town-officers of Winchester performed the like services on the line of said towns Nov. 15; and again those of Royalston and Warwick did the same between their towns Nov. 16.

During the first year of the war, the town in its corporate capacity did not take any action in the matter: but July 28, 1862, the town voted to instruct the selectmen to offer a bounty of $100 to each volunteer to the number of thirteen; also voted to instruct the selectmen to petition the next General Court to pass an act legalizing the assessment of said bounty upon the polls and estates of the inhabitants of the town.

Aug. 25, 1862. — Voted to authorize the selectmen to offer a bounty of $100 to each person who shall volunteer and be accepted to fill the quota of the town on the last call for 300,000 men by the President.

Voted to authorize the selectmen to borrow money for the before-named purpose.

Also voted to instruct the selectmen to petition the next General Court for the assessment of the same upon the polls and estates of the inhabitants of the town.

December, 1862. — The town received the present of a bell from Col. McKim (his wife is a daughter of Col. Lemuel Wheelock, a former resident of this town). Said bell was suspended from the dome of the village schoolhouse, as wished by the donor, and dedicated by a public meeting, with appropriate speeches from several of the citizens of our town, expressing their gratitude to the giver for his valuable and very useful gift.*

* See Appendix, page 190.

Feb. 17, 1863. — Deacon Hervey Barber gave a lecture in the evening, giving some of the more important events in the past history of the town (it being the centennial anniversary of its incorporation), in the Unitarian church, which was heard by a large and attentive audience. March 2. — The town voted to empower the treasurer, with the approbation of the selectmen, to borrow money to be expended as aid to families of volunteers. Amount paid to twenty-two volunteers previous to March 2, 1863, $2,202.78. April 2. — The town voted on the following amendment to the Constitution of the Commonwealth; viz., "No person of foreign birth shall be entitled to vote, or shall be eligible to office, until he shall have resided within the jurisdiction of the United States for two years subsequent to having received his naturalization-papers, and shall be otherwise qualified as required by the Constitution and laws of this Commonwealth." The votes being received and counted, there were 40 yeas; nays, none.

Dec. 12, 1863. — Voted to authorize the selectmen to procure volunteers for the United-States service.

April 6, 1864. — Voted to raise the sum of $1,500, to be assessed, or as much of the same as the selectmen shall deem necessary, to be expended in the payment of bounties to soldiers who have volunteered or shall volunteer on the town's quota.

June 13, 1864. — Voted to raise the sum of $624 to indemnify the selectmen for moneys expended in furnishing recruits for the United-States service, the same to be assessed the present year; also voted to instruct the selectmen to fill by enlistment of recruits all future quotas of said town on future calls previous to a draft being made or ordered; also voted to authorize the selectmen to borrow money for the same.

What follows was taken from Adj.-Gen. Schouler's "History of Massachusetts in the Civil War," vol. ii. Warwick incorporated Feb. 17, 1763. Population in 1860, 932; in 1865, 909. Valuation in 1860, $342,556; in 1865, $220,657.

The selectmen in 1861 and 1862 were William H. Bass, Sylvanus N. Atwood, Charles R. Gale; in 1863, Charles R. Gale, Hervey Barber, Eben G. Ball; in 1864, Hervey Barber, Eben G. Ball, Jesse F. Bridge; in 1865, E. F. Mayo, J. F. Bridge, William H. Gale.

The town-clerk during all these years of the war was Edward F. Mayo. The town-treasurer in 1861, 1862, and 1863, was Benjamin G. Putnam; in 1864 and 1865, Philip Young.

Mr. Mayo, the town-clerk, writes, "The men who went from our town were among our best citizens; and those that have returned to us fully occupy their former stations. We have lost in the war twenty-six men. Alexander Cooper, sergeant of Company G, Thirty-sixth Regiment Massachusetts Volunteers, was more than three years in the army, and was discharged for wounds received at Spottsylvania. He was killed Nov. 22, 1866, by the fall of a derrick, while raising a stone for the soldiers' monument in this town."

Warwick furnished ninety-nine men for the war; which was a surplus of nine above all demands.

April 6, 1864. — The town voted to accept of the grant of land given by Mrs. Experience C. Fisk for an addition to our burying-ground, complying with the conditions of said grant. Also voted that the Chair appoint a committee of three persons to draft suitable resolutions, expressing the gratitude of the town to the donor, and report to this meeting; the same to be presented to Mrs. Fisk, and a copy to be inscribed on the records of the town.

Rev. I. S. Lincoln, William H. Bass, and Deacon G. W. Moore were nominated by H. Barber, chairman, and confirmed by the town. Then voted that the selectmen be a committee to examine the grounds, and report at a future meeting. The committee to draft resolutions, &c., reported as follows : —

Whereas, As Mrs. Experience C. Fisk presented to the town of Warwick a beautiful and valuable lot of land contiguous to the existing cemetery : therefore

Resolved, That the citizens of said town receive the same with gratitude, and, in town-meeting assembled, return a vote of thanks to the donor for her most valuable and acceptable gift.

Resolved, That this land thus received, and consecrated as a resting-place for the dead, shall be called the Fisk Cemetery.

Resolved, That the town-clerk is hereby instructed to place this preamble and resolutions upon the town-records, and present the same to the donor, and send a copy thereof to the editor of " The Gazette and Courier " at Greenfield, for publication.

I. S. LINCOLN, \
G. W. MOORE, } *Committee.* \
W. H. BASS, /

WARWICK, April 6, 1865.

The selectmen, being chosen a committee for that purpose, examined the grounds given by Mrs. Fisk, and reported that said grounds needed fencing on three sides; that some parts needed levelling; that several old trees should be cut down, and the old cellar be filled up; that walks and driveways should be made, and that it should be otherwise beautified, to comply with the wishes of the donor.

HERVEY BARBER,
E. G. BALL, } Committee.
J. F. BRIDGE,

Report accepted by the town; and the selectmen were instructed to carry the substance of said report into effect.

The above improvements were made during the season; and several times since the town has directed their selectmen to make further alterations; so that when the ornamental trees have become some larger, and all vacant places that were at first proposed for trees of various kinds are filled, the Fisk Cemetery will compare favorably with any in this vicinity.

1865. — As per report of the overseers of the poor, the sum-total of expense of paupers on the town the past year is $121.35.

Whole number of weeks' board of paupers on the town-farm was 364.

Average cost of board per week, $33\frac{1}{3}$ cents each.

Whole expense of the farm, $141.70.

Sum-total of expense for the year, $263.05.

HERVEY BARBER, } Overseers of the Poor.
JESSE F. BRIDGE,

WARWICK, March 4, 1865.

A small expense per week for the support of persons on the town-farm, which speaks favorably for the way we support our paupers, and the manner that we proceed in cultivating the farm, and superintending the whole concern.

This year there died at Whately (at the residence of her son, Samuel Lesure, Esq.) Mrs. Hannah Lesure, widow of Mr. Samuel Lesure, aged 101 years, 4 months, and 12 days. Samuel Lesure, sen., was one of the first settlers of the town of Warwick, and was a soldier in the war of the Revolution, and for some years a pensioner. His widow received a pension also after the decease of her husband until the time of her departure to that "better land." We will now record a traditionary anecdote, related by one of her contemporaries, which may interest the younger portion of our readers.

While her husband was absent in the service of his country, between the years 1780 and 1783, Mrs. Lesure espied one evening in the twilight, in the edge of the woods near her dwelling-house, a large bear, coolly taking a survey of the log-house and its surroundings. And, knowing that bears have a particular penchant for pigs, she immediately took hers from the pen, and put it in the house; closed the door, and barricaded it with table, stools, and blocks, and other movables that the dwelling contained; put her large fire-shovel into the embers; and patiently waited the result. Soon Bruin made his assault upon the door, and she could plainly see his nose under the door, which was hung on wooden hinges, also fastened with a wooden latch, and a string, for the purpose of opening, suspended from the outside,—locks at that time being almost unknown. The floor being laid with loose boards, the door fitted none of the best. But, not being able to force an entrance, he next went to the slide board-window (glass at that time was very scarce), which, in her haste, she had neglected to fasten. This he soon forced open enough to admit his head, when our heroine seized the shovel, and made such an onslaught upon the head of the bear, that he soon retreated to the woods with growls and snarls, and left our hostess and her lodger in quiet possession of her humble abode. And when Mrs. Lesure was over a hundred years of age, she showed both her ability to labor and her patriotism by knitting stockings for our soldiers that had left their homes to sustain our government when threatened by traitors belonging to the slaveholders' rebellion.

1866. — See account of the building of the soldiers' monument, which contains all the votes of the town, except those usually recorded every year.*

March 4, 1867. — The town voted to authorize the treasurer, with the approbation of the selectmen, to borrow money for the support of the families of volunteers, disabled soldiers, and the families of the slain; and the same vote has been passed at the annual March meeting each year from that time to the present.

Nov. 3, 1868. — Town voted to pay Andrew F. Norton his town bounty ($125), with interest, from the date of his enlistment as a soldier accredited to Warwick in the war of the late Rebellion.

Norton's name, with several others, had been before

* On pages 146–149.

the town, and the selectmen as a committee to investigate the subject, for over two years. The others failed to receive their bounty, not from any neglect of duty, but from being unfortunate in the time of enlistment, it being prior to the date of the act making it legal for towns to pay the above bounty.

1869. — The legislature of the Commonwealth passed an act abolishing the school-district system.

April 17. — The town voted to choose a committee to appraise the school-houses, and report at a future meeting; then voted that the selectmen (James S. Wheeler, E. F. Mayo, and H. H. Jillson) be said committee. Also voted, and added George N. Richards and William H. Bass to the committee.

And voted to adjourn this meeting to May 15, at three o'clock, P.M., to hear the report of said committee.

May 15. — The inhabitants met agreeably to adjournment; heard the report of the committee on the appraisal of school-houses, and voted to lay the report over to the next March meeting.

Sept. 6, 1870. — The town voted unanimously to accept of the act, and return to the school-district system.

Nov. 8. — Voted to appropriate $100 for the benefit of a public library. Also voted to accept of the two pieces of land north of Nahum Jones's boot-shop; the same to be kept as a public park, and to be kept enclosed with a suitable and substantial fence. And also voted that the selectmen be a committee to dispose of the timber on the town-farm, if, in their opinion, it would be for the best interests of the town.

The proprietors of the park, prior to the above vote, were several citizens of the town, who had authorized their committee to convey said park to the town, on condition that the town would vote to receive it, and forever after keep it in suitable repair, as an ornament to the village. Its history is as follows. Some time in August, 1867, Mrs. M. A. McKim (a former resident of Warwick), Mrs. E. C. Sibley, and Miss Sarah Ball, circulated a subscription-paper for the purpose of purchasing the blacksmith-shop lot, north of Mrs. McKim's new house in Warwick Village, and Mr. Jones's lot, north of his boot-shop, to be improved and ornamented for a public park. On said subscription-paper are to be found the names of our citizens to the amount of $325, for the purpose of purchasing said pieces of land. After said facts had become known, Mr. Jones generously presented his lot, and gave a deed thereof to the town ; and the blacksmith lot was purchased of A. S. Atherton, Mrs. McKim being the original owner. They each gave $25 for the above object. The proprietors, or rather the contributors, met at the hotel, and voted to choose a committee of three persons from their number to take charge of the funds contributed, and finish off and beautify said grounds in a suitable manner for a public park. Voted and chose Hervey Barber, Calvin W. Delva, and Edward F. Mayo, said committee, who circulated another paper for subscriptions for the above purpose ; and they obtained the promise on the same of the sum of $127.50, to be paid in money, labor, and materials, as specified on said paper, to be expended under the supervision of the committee, for the purpose of levelling, fencing, the setting of trees, and otherwise ornamenting said park. The committee soon commenced their work; and after some delays, from one cause and another, the more prominent one being the want of funds, and the county-commissioners having laid a road in such a way as to necessitate the selectmen to take a part of the proprietors' lands for the continuance and extension of said road, the lot, being fenced and nearly finished, was presented to the town, and accepted, as above stated, and a deed of warranty given by Messrs. Jones and Atherton, on condition that the town ever after keep the same in good order, and continue it as a public park.

March 6, 1871. — The town voted to accept of the proprietors' library, on the following conditions: That the town shall, at the annual March meeting each year, choose a board of five trustees, who shall have power to appoint a librarian, to furnish a suitable place to keep the library, to make by-laws, and adopt such regulations for its government and support as they in their judgment shall think best. Said trustees shall have power to fill all vacancies which may occur by reason of death, removal, or otherwise, during the year. They shall report to the town at the annual March meeting their doings and the condition of the library. And the town shall, from time to time, make such appropriations as shall be necessary to increase the number of volumes, and thereby increase the usefulness of the library. And, when the town shall fail to comply with the conditions on which they receive the library, it shall revert to the original owners. The town voted, and chose as trustees of the library Rev. John Goldsbury, Deacon H. Barber, Dr. S. P. French, Jesse F. Bridge, Esq., and William K. Taylor. Also voted to appropriate the money returned to the town by the county-treasurer, from the dog-tax, to the library; to be expended by the trustees for the benefit of the same.

April 10. — The town voted to accept a donation of $500, given by Mrs. Mary Blake Clap, of Dorchester District, Boston, and comply with the request of the donor, which was as follows : " That said sum shall be invested by the town, and the interest arising therefrom shall be annually applied to the beautifying and keeping their cemetery in repair."

Also voted that the town-clerk and selectmen constitute a committee to draft suitable resolutions, the same to be presented to Mrs. Clap, and also to be inscribed upon the records of the town, expressing the gratitude of the town to the donor for her very acceptable gift.

The committee presented the following report, which was accepted by the town : —

Preamble. — The undersigned having been chosen by the citizens of the town of Warwick, in town-meeting assembled, to make and transmit to Mrs. Mary Blake Clap, of Boston, an expression of thanks, and the grateful acknowledgment thereof of the people of this town for her generous action in aid of our cemetery : therefore

Resolved, That we herewith present to Mrs. Mary Blake Clap, of Boston, the grateful thanks of the town for her very generous donation to the town as a cemetery-fund.

Resolved, That it is our intention to carry out the wishes expressed by the donor, and comply with them in such a manner as to make the spot endeared to us as the last resting-place of the bodies of our relatives and friends a pleasant rather than a gloomy retreat.

ARNON S. ATHERTON, *Town-Clerk.*

E. F. MAYO,
H. H. JILLSON, } *Selectmen.*
J. F. BRIDGE,

May 2. — The town voted to prohibit the sale of ale, porter, strong and lager beer, within the limits of the town the ensuing year.

Nov. 7. — Voted that the matter concerning school-districts in the warrant be referred to the chairman of the school-committee and the selectmen, who shall take the subject into consideration, and report at some future meeting.

March 4, 1872. — Voted, and chose William H. Gale moderator; also Henry H. Jillson, Jesse F. Bridge, and James L. Stockwell, selectmen, and assessors, and overseers of poor; A. S. Atherton, town-clerk and treasurer; George A. Cushing, superintending school-committee for three years; Nahum Jones, Hervey Barber, Dr. French, Jesse F. Bridge, and William K. Taylor, trustees of the public library; William K. Taylor, constable, and collector of taxes.

Also voted to accept of the report of the selectmen, which leaves a balance of $8,450.93, as the indebtedness of the town above all resources.

Voted to raise two per cent on the valuation, which shall constitute, with the amount assessed upon the polls, the sum-total of the State, county, and town taxes the present year.

Voted to appropriate, out of the above, $1,200 for the use of the schools the ensuing year.

Voted to appropriate $100 to be expended by the trustees for the enlargement of the town-library.

Voted to raise one-half per cent on the valuation, which shall, with the poll-taxes, be the amount to be expended on the highways the coming year.

Voted to continue the school-district system. Also voted to hear the report of the committee raised at a former meeting to take into consideration our school-districts, and make such alteration therein as may be to the best interests of the town, which was as follows, to wit : —

The subscribers chosen by the town as a committee to make such alterations in the bounds of several school-districts have attended to that duty, and ask leave to submit the following report : —

Your committee are of the opinion that it will be for the interest of the town, and not add much to the inconvenience of the inhabitants of said districts, to annex the lands and estates of Mrs. Stratton, George W. Smith, Luke Delvee, Henry Esketh, and the Messrs. Holden, in school-district No. 6, to district No. 4 ; and unite the remaining lands and estates of school-district No. 6 with school-district No. 3, to be called school-district No. 6, — its original number ; also unite school-district No. 10 with No. 7, to be continued as No. 7 ; also that district No. 9 take the name of No. 3, — its former number ; — making eight districts within the town, numbered from one to eight in regular order. And we are of the opinion that any further alterations would be inexpedient at the present time. All of which is submitted for the consideration of the town.

HERVEY BARBER,
E. F. MAYO, } *Committee.*
J. F. BRIDGE,

WARWICK, Feb. 10, 1872.

Also voted to accept of the report of the Rev. John Goldsbury for the trustees of the town-library; and ordered the same to be printed with the report of the school-committee, for the use of the inhabitants of the town.

And the trustees at their annual meeting passed a vote of thanks to the Rev. Mr. Goldsbury for his able, instructive, and interesting report, and ordered it inscribed on the records of the library.

S. P. FRENCH, *Secretary.*

April 20, 1872. — At a town-meeting held for the purpose, it was voted to accept of a second donation of $500 from Mrs. Mary Blake Clap for the improvement of the cemetery, and comply with the wishes of the donor; and that the selectmen and town-clerk present to her the thanks of the town for her acceptable and desirable gift.

A. S. ATHERTON, *Town-Clerk.*

THE REBELLION OF 1861-1865.

The outbreak of the war of the Rebellion, and a call for troops to defend the national capital, although not unexpected by our people, was nevertheless something of a surprise, as we had for many years lived in peace, and knew very little of the waste of life, of time, and of treasure, which a state of war entails upon a community therein engaged. At this time, and for many years previous, no military organization existed in our town; and our whole number of enrolled militia consisted of less than one hundred and fifty men between the ages of eighteen and forty-five years, of which more than one-half were invalids, or in some way incompetent to do military duty. Yet on the part of our citizens, both old and young, male and female, there was shown a persevering determination to support the government in putting down the Rebellion by enlisting their energies in sustaining the stars and stripes, and maintaining to the last the union of all the States of our beloved country, as the brief history of what we shall say of the doings of our patriotic people during those years of labor, suspense, and trial, will fully corroborate; and which shows our readiness and willingness to sacrifice time, wealth, and even life, in our country's defence.

We would first record, that soon after the assault upon Fort Sumter, before any calls had been made upon our town for troops, a large number of our young men had enlisted, and gone to the front to assist in sustaining the authorities in maintaining the rights of all American citizens,—liberty, freedom, and a strong republican government. Although the majority of them were not afterwards accredited to our town, yet those that remained rejoiced to see so many of their companions and neighbors showing their patriotism by giving themselves to the cause of the free institutions of their beloved republic, which were now threatened by their deluded Southern countrymen,—a strong evidence to those that remained that the principles of justice, right, and freedom, would ultimately prevail. And several times during the war large contributions of clothing, bandages, lint, and palatable kinds of preserves, fruits, and food, were collected by the noble women of our town, and sent to the hospitals for the comfort and subsistence of our sick and wounded soldiers, who were suffering and dying to sustain the best government on the face of the earth. And often were the manly forms of our fathers and sons collected together to sustain and cheer each other, as doubt and hope came over the wires with lightning-speed, announcing first defeat and then victory to their inquiring and anxious minds, as they were looking for news from the army of occupation or of advance into the enemy's country. And quite often large subscriptions were collected to aid the government in forwarding men to the front, as they were called for from time to time. The whole amount of money appropriated and expended by the town on account of the war, exclusive of State aid, was $8,786.09. There was also raised by private subscription $2,638.21, which was not reimbursed by the town.

The amount of money raised and expended by the town, for State aid to soldiers' families during the years of the war, and which was afterwards reimbursed by the Commonwealth, was $6,403.07, making a sum-total of $17,827.37, which was raised by our patriotic citizens during those years, besides large amounts of articles of various kinds sent for the relief of our sick and wounded soldiers.*

THE SOLDIERS' MONUMENT.

Nov. 7, 1865, the town voted to erect a monument to the memory of its deceased soldiers who fell in the war of the slaveholders' rebellion.

Also voted that the selectmen be instructed to obtain drafts and plans for a monument, and submit them to the town at some future meeting.

And voted that the committee be confined to granite as the material for building said monument.

March 5, 1866, voted to authorize the selectmen to contract for furnishing the material for the erection of a suitable monument to the memory of its deceased soldiers, and to authorize said selectmen to borrow a sum of money, not exceeding $1,000, for the same.

Aug. 25, the town voted to have the soldiers' monument erected in the Fisk Cemetery.

During this season a beautiful granite monument was purchased by the selectmen, and transported

* See Appendix, page 189.

from the quarry in Fitzwilliam, N.H., and placed in the centre of the Fisk Cemetery, on suitable and substantial foundations,— a memorial to the patriotism of our sons, to the number of twenty-six,* whose names are inscribed thereon, and will show to future generations the gratitude of all our citizens; that they so nobly gave their lives to their country in the suppression of the greatest rebellion ever known, thereby showing to the world that republican institutions are revered, preserving the Union, abolishing African slavery, enlarging the freedom of all, and leaving our land in a situation to become the greatest, the wisest, and the happiest upon the face of the earth.

And we are happy to record, that as yet no one has expressed any dissatisfaction that this memento to the worth of our lamented sons has been erected to perpetuate their prowess and patriotism. But many there are who rejoice that they have, in this commendable manner, commemorated their disinterestedness and valor. A tribute of respect is due to those of our fellow-citizens who gave their influence to forward the object, and especially to the selectmen who acted for the town in its corporate capacity, and those friends that still have a deep interest in the prosperity of their former and ever-to-be-remembered residence, and who so generously contributed towards its completion, in a sum of $336, which, with the town's grant of $1,000, makes $1,336, which is the total expense of erecting and finishing

---

* See names in Appendix, page 189.

both the monument and the grounds surrounding the same.

In addition to what has already been said of the minerals in this town, we would say that the radiated tourmaline, found in large quantities on Mt. Gràce, is one of the handsomest of its kind; and there are specimens of it to be found in many of the cabinets of mineralogists in this country, and in several in the Old World. From the quarry of crystallized quartz found near the road leading from the Common in Warwick towards C. W. Hastings's pond, on lands of Widow Rhoda Wheelock, are obtained noble specimens, which are quite extensively known and appreciated by many professors both in our country and in Europe; and Prof. Tenney has a splendid impression of a specimen of this mineral, to be found in his valuable work on mineralogy. We will also continue the account of the natural curiosities in town by a brief statement of an Indian kettle that will hold from eight to ten pails of water, to be found on the south side of a ledge of rocks on the west side of the road, about a hundred rods northwest of Chandler W. Bass's saw-mill; and of a bear's den, so called, on the Nath. G. Stevens farm, not far from a hundred rods north of the Stevens's millpond, and from twenty to thirty rods east of the line between Northfield and Warwick: this den is covered by a shelving rock of a size sufficient to shelter five hundred men. Also, on Mr. D. Stone's Atwood farm, on the west side of the old road, near the Winchester line, is to be found a large bowlder, adjudged to weigh a hundred tons, which is so nearly balanced that it can be rocked with one hand. These things are richly worth the time and trouble of a journey of some distance to any lover of natural curiosities.

AGRICULTURE.

For the last twenty years the farming interests of the town have somewhat improved: the inhabitants have become convinced that science and system are as necessary to success as bone and muscle; and most of our farmers have adopted the plan of cultivating a smaller number of acres, and by a rotation of crops, and a higher state of improvement, obtain a better return for their labor.

Their attention is more devoted to the raising of fruit, hay, and vegetables than formerly. Some have planted new orchards, and others have trimmed and grafted their old ones; quite a quantity of the best varieties of apples are now grown, so that in ordinary years they have enough for their own supply, and in fruitful ones an overplus to carry to market. The number of horses, cattle, sheep, and swine, has decreased more than half; but, as they consist of better grades and larger forms, their value has increased, while their numbers have been continually decreasing

Their dwellings are more comfortable and elegant, their fences improved, and their carriages and farming-tools show a utility never before dreamed of, and their value has increased over a hundred per cent. There is also an appearance of neatness and thrift to be seen about their homes never before known since the memory of our oldest inhabitants; and around many of their dwellings are now planted ornamental trees, interspersed with flowers and other things of taste, which, in some instances, make the passers remark that these people have much to make them comfortable and happy.

CATTLE-SHOWS AND FAIRS.

In the autumns of 1859 and 1860 the people of this town held a cattle-show on the Common, and a fair in the Unitarian Church, each year, which were attended by a large number of the inhabitants of Warwick; and nearly all the towns within twenty miles were represented by quite a respectable number of their best citizens: and many brought with them specimens of their agricultural products, and manufactured articles, while others presented their best horses, neat cattle, sheep, and swine; and we had natural curiosities, flowers, paintings, and other articles of the fine arts; and, in fact, about every thing that is ever exhibited on similar occasions. We also, at our first gathering, had an able extempore address from R. D. Chase, Esq., of Orange, on the benefits that we should derive from a continuation of these meetings in after years. At our meeting together on the second occasion, W. Griswold, Esq., of Greenfield, gave us an interesting and instructive scientific address, interspersed with anecdotes and other matter, so suitably arranged as to give general satisfaction.

We felt that our cattle-shows and fairs had become quite a success; and we only regret that we have been unable to continue them to this time, as we are satisfied, that, had we done so, it would have been for the advancement of the knowledge of agricultural science, and suggested improvements in practical farming generally.

MANUFACTURES.

The manufacturing interests of our town are comparatively small, for the reasons that have already been stated; yet with the perseverance and industry of our people they are nevertheless considerable. They consist mostly of lumber of various kinds, or of such articles as are made from lumber, or of which wood is the component part.

In the first place, we would mention that we have fourteen saw-mills within the limits of the town, two of temporary steam-power: nine of them have circular saws of the most approved structure; and they, all combined, cut out over four million of feet of lumber annually, consisting of pine, chestnut, hemlock, and hard wood, which is carried to the dépôts in the adjoining towns, and transported by steam-cars on the railroads to all parts of New England, and the State of New York. It is worth at the dépôts, when placed on the cars, on an average, over fifteen dollars per thousand. The whole process of cutting, hauling, manufacturing, and carting to the railroads, employs a large number of men in the winter season, and some during the other seasons of the year. We also have nine smaller mills, that cut pail-staves, chair-stuff, shingles, and broom-handles in considerable quantities, which also find a market abroad.

The stave-mills the past year cut staves and heading for over one hundred and fifty thousand pails. And, besides the above, a large amount of wood is cut from our hills and valleys, and hauled to Winchester, Northfield, and Wendell, to be used by the inhabitants of these places, or sold to the railroad companies for their use, or transportation to other less wooded regions.

We have also a tannery that employs eight men manufacturing upper leather. They use three hundred cords of hemlock bark annually. This bark is mostly grown in town, and is worth from eight to ten dollars a cord. The annual product of this tannery is over fifty tons of leather, — worth, when ready for market, over twenty thousand dollars.

In the village is a boot manufactory, which has been in operation eighteen years. The business was established by Nahum Jones (then a resident of Boston, now of Warwick). It was commenced on a small scale, and has gradually increased from about fifteen thousand dollars to fifty thousand dollars per annum, and gives employment to forty men in the various departments of the business. The number of pairs of men's, boys', and youths' boots made here in 1871 was twenty thousand. These boots are adapted to the New-England trade. Nearly all the men employed are residents of the town, and owners of real estate.

In the south part of the town is quite a large shop for the manufacture of brush-woods formerly owned by James S. Wheeler (deceased), but now by his son. They make and send to market over twenty-five hundred gross of brush-woods annually. These woods are made of hard wood, and employ from six to eight men; and the annual product is from four thousand dollars to six thousand dollars, as the season proves to be wet or dry, the power used being water. And there are several small shops that manufacture quite a large amount of chair-stuff of various kinds.

THE WARWICK LIGHT INFANTRY.

In the year 1852 the citizens of Warwick, to the number of fifty or over, united for the purpose of forming themselves into a military company, and petitioned the authorities of the State for powers and privileges given by them to other similar organizations.

Their request was heard, and soon answered; and a charter was granted for five years under the name of the Warwick Light Infantry, allowing them such recompense for their services as other infantry-companies received, on condition that they well and truly performed all the duties required of them by the statutes of the Commonwealth.

Said company assembled, and elected James Stockwell captain, Edward F. Mayo and Henry G. Mallard lieutenants, with all other officers that were necessary to make them an efficient company of volunteer militia.

This company was armed and equipped in a becoming and tasteful manner, and performed all the military duties that the law required for the full term of their charter with a faithful and soldier-like precision, first under Capt. Stockwell, afterwards under Capts. Mayo and Mallard, so as to receive the approbation of their superior officers, and the esteem of their fellow-citizens. And several times have I heard it remarked by the spectators who witnessed their soldierly appearance, and the accuracy of their evolutions, "that such a company was an honor to any town."

THE CORNET BAND.

For twenty years our town has been *cheered* and made *happier* by the *harmony of sweet sounds*, called forth by an organized body of our citizens called the Warwick Cornet Band. Said organization commenced its operations under Charles F. Hastings as leader, which in a few years was transferred to James E. Fuller, and for a few months to Edward F. Mayo, who with their great love of music, and their usual promptitude of action, soon drew around them a dozen or more of our young men of *musical talent*, who, mostly under their instruction (with occasionally a teacher from abroad), developed so much skill in the science of music, that for several years they were considered an important element in all our public gatherings, and a great source of pleasure to the citizens of Warwick as they met from week to week for practice, either on the town common or in the band-room, and united their efforts to become masters of *the sweetest, the highest*, the most soul-cheering power ever given to man.

They were often invited to the neighboring towns to assist at their fairs, picnics, and other places of amusement and pleasure; where they were efficient in calling forth such harmonious strains of excellent music, that, after their return to their homes, they were followed with gratitude from those whose happiness was enhanced; and we were congratulated for our accomplished band of excellent musicians.

For several years past, the band has been continued under the leadership of Mr. Samuel Hastings, who has and does still give much time and zeal to the work, as the members have been continually changing, so that at the present time but a very few remain that belonged to the company when he was first chosen to be its leader and teacher; and we are happy to record that all the expressions of gratitude and praise given by any one to its first leader and his comrades can, with equal sincerity, be given to him and those with whom he is associated. In fact, the band has become so much of a fixture, that if we should be deprived of its services, even for a short time, our gatherings of all kinds would be exceedingly tame, if we were obliged to meet without seeing their smiling faces, or hearing their sweet, melodious sounds; and we would here add, for ourselves, and the citizens of our town, to the "Warwick Cornet Band," as it now is, and as it has been, an expression of thanks, to be handed to coming generations with this work, that their children and ours may know that their labors of love are appreciated by us, and those that immediately preceded us.

We hope that the present members will persevere in their noble work, and that those that come after them and have like talents will be moved by their example and perseverance to come forward and do likewise. And we feel assured that their contemporaries will shower blessings of gratitude upon their heads.

SCHOOLS.

Our schools have been, for some years, considered by our neighbors as good as any to be found in this vicinity. Although we have never had a sufficient number of inhabitants to oblige the town to maintain a high-school, yet the desire that our children and youth should receive a good practical education has been so great, that, for a series of years, we have succeeded in sustaining one of a private nature, or, in other words, a select school, where the higher branches could be learned; and, at other times, many of our young men and women have gone one or two terms each year to schools and academies in the adjoining towns; so that, for the last forty years, we have not only been able to supply our own schools with competent teachers, but have also supplied several to the neighboring towns. And, in the year 1840, during the winter term, twelve young gentlemen and several young ladies, natives of Warwick, taught school in this and the adjoining towns. For the past few years, the number of scholars attending school has been reduced more than fifty per cent, and some of our schools are very small: yet the interest taken in them has in no way declined, nor our schools, as a whole, deteriorated, as the town-grant of $1,200 for that purpose amply proves; and we feel assured, by what we see and hear, that our people, as a class, are determined that their children shall enjoy for time to come still greater facilities of obtaining a good, practical, common-school education than were given to those of former years, being convinced that our common schools are the only sure foundation of a free government.

HISTORY OF ITS CHURCHES CONTINUED.

THE FIRST CONGREGATIONAL (NOW UNITARIAN) CHURCH.

As has already been recorded by the Hon. Jona. Blake, the Rev. Preserved Smith was ordained Oct. 12, 1814, and continued as pastor of this church and society for thirty years; and, for this series of years, he not only performed all his church and parochial duties, as a faithful minister, a devoted Christian, and an exemplary man, but he was also first and foremost in all things that would in any way advance the true interests of his people, or would further, and be instrumental in, the happiness and progress of all the inhabitants of the town. Especially have his influence and example been witnessed in the advancement and prosperity of our common schools; and we feel that we are justified in recording, that, to him more than any other man, are we indebted for the high standard to which they attained during his long residence among us as our teacher and guide. He asked of us and obtained his dismission in 1844, and preached his farewell sermon Oct. 12 of the same year. After the lapse of twenty years, he came, by request of his still grateful people, Oct. 12, 1864, and delivered his half-century discourse to a large, attentive, and interested audience.

The order of exercises was as follows: —

1. Voluntary by the choir, E. F. Mayo, leader.

2. Reading of Scriptures by Rev. John Goldsbury of Warwick.

3. Hymn of Welcome. Original. By Miss M. A. Reed of Warwick (now wife of Rev. H. P. Osgood).*

4. Prayer by Rev. J. F. Moors of Greenfield.

5. Hymn from "Greenwood's Collection," read by Rev. S. Barber.

6. Sermon. Text from Acts xxvi. 22, "Having obtained help of God, I continue to this day."

7. Prayer by Rev. Alpheus Harding of New Salem.

8. Farewell Hymn. Original. By Miss M. A. Reed.

9. Benediction by Rev. I. S. Lincoln, resident pastor.

After the services in the church, there was a col-

---

* See Appendix, p. 205.

lation in the vestry, at which there were remarks by both clergymen and laymen, closing with dismission-hymn. The church was very tastefully decorated with flowers and emblems appropriate to the occasion. Mr. Smith is now (March 16, 1872) residing in Greenfield, enjoying a comfortable measure of health.

We will here quote an extract from Rev. Mr. Smith, where he speaks of the generation that were leaders in the church, and worthy citizens of the town at the time of his settlement.

"There was the sainted Barnes, whose walk was with God; J. Blake, sen., was truly, in dress and manners, a gentleman of the old school; Dea. Caleb Mayo, noted for his straightforward uprightness and integrity; Capt. Peter Proctor, the unflinching patriot; Capt. Mark Moore, the substantial friend of good order; and women not a few, who were mothers in Israel, full of good works, and ministrations of mercy and kindness." Also, "In 1831, Warwick was visited by a dysentery of a very malignant type, which swept off, in about seven weeks, sixteen persons, old and young. In the families of John Whitney, jun., and John Bowman, four died out of each within a few days. Mr. Bowman's sister and child were buried at one time: at another, a week after, he himself and another child were buried at the same time."

Rev. D. H. Barlow supplied the desk in 1845, 1846, and 1847, a part of the time, but resided in town only a part of the time. Rev. Samuel F. Clark in 1848, one half of the time, and in Athol the other part, where he was settled the following year. Rev. George F.

Clark was installed as pastor of this church April 14, 1848. Rev. F. T. Gray of Boston preached the sermon; Rev. O. C. Everett of Northfield made the installing prayer; Rev. S. F. Clark of Athol gave the right hand of fellowship. He was dismissed April 1, 1852. After his dismission, Rev. Luther Wilson of Petersham supplied till April 1, 1854. Rev. Abraham Jackson of Walpole, N.H., supplied from April 1, 1854, to April 1, 1855. The Rev. John Goldsbury commenced to supply in 1856, and continued to April 1, 1859. The Rev. Increase S. Lincoln commenced his ministry in September, 1860, and closed his labors for this church in June, 1867. The Rev. J. B. Willard of Harvard supplied through the summer and autumn of 1867. From that time to Sept. 20, 1868, the pulpit was supplied by different clergymen. The Rev. William A. P. Willard commenced his labors Sept. 20, 1868, and was ordained as pastor of this church and society Jan. 20, 1869. The services on that occasion were as follows: Invocation by Rev. M. Baker of Orange. Reading of the Scriptures by Rev. J. Goldsbury of Warwick. Sermon by Rev. J. F. Moors of Greenfield. Ordaining prayer by Rev. J. B. Willard of Harvard. Charge by Rev. S. Barber of Bernardston. Right hand of fellowship by Rev. I. S. Lincoln of Winchester, N.H. Address to the people by Rev. Mr. Baker of Orange. Benediction by the pastor-elect. The singing, under the direction of Capt. E. F. Mayo, was in fine taste; and its departing strains will linger upon the ear a long time. The church was wreathed, arched, and garlanded with evergreens, in a style that did credit to the managers.

April 1, 1870, Mr. Willard tendered his resignation to the church, to take effect Oct. 1, 1870. Resignation accepted by the church, and by the society soon after. Since that time the church has been destitute of a pastor, but has been supplied by the Rev. John Goldsbury of Warwick for the former, and the Rev. Mr. Bailey of Athol for the latter part of the time. Unitarian preachers originating from Warwick: Rev. John Goldsbury, Rev. Nathan Ball, Rev. Amory Gale, Rev. Stillman Barber, Rev. Amory D. Mayo, and the Rev. Henry H. Barber.

Their church edifice (as has been said) was erected in 1836, and was first painted and repaired in 1846 by Joshua T. Sanger, under the superintendence of Ira Draper, Caleb M. Proctor, and James Stockwell, a committee chosen for the purpose, who assessed $150 upon the pews to defray the expenses of said repairs. Mr. Sanger was faithful to his trust; and his work was performed in a substantial and acceptable manner.

In 1859, after the church had been considerably damaged by a stroke of lightning, a committee was elected, consisting of Ira Draper, Hervey Barber, and N. E. Stevens, to superintend the repairs upon the same, who were instructed to assess a sufficient sum upon the pews in said church to defray the expenses thereof, not exceeding $300. Said committee contracted with Mr. John Turner of Orange, for the sum of $258, to perform the above services, and assessed $269 upon the pews to pay the same, and other contingent expenses thereof.

Again, in 1870, the parish voted to raise $500 for

the purpose of new shingling, painting, and repairing their church ; and a committee was elected, consisting of Samuel W. Spooner, Hervey Barber, and Edward F. Mayo, who were instructed to assess so much of the above sum as would be sufficient to pay the repairs of all kinds upon the outside of the building ; while the papering, and other ornamenting of the inside, was to be raised by subscription, or in some other way that might be devised. Said committee assessed $434.52 upon the pews, and employed the Messrs. Graves Brothers of Amherst (by the day) to paint and ornament, and William K. Taylor to shingle and repair, said church.

Said committee by their treasurer (Hervey Barber) collected the above $434.52, and received of E. F. Mayo $284.02, a balance of the proceeds of two prior fairs, or levees, raised by the ladies of the society for the purpose of doing the ornamental work on the inside of their church; and nearly $100 by donation from William B. Spooner of Boston, Rev. Mr. White of Keene, N.H., the Unitarian society at Springfield, Mrs. Merrifield, and others ; and $60 as the proceeds of lectures given by Rev. A. D. Mayo, Rev. J. F. Moors, and Rev. H. H. Barber, — the balance from other sources making a sum-total of $1,067.83 as the expense of said repairs, which is now (March, 1872) all settled and paid : so that they not only have a well-proportioned church, but one that is completely and elegantly finished ; and they now have as neat, tastefully-arranged, and beautiful a church as can be seen in any of the adjoining towns.

April 1, 1864, Mrs. M ( ) (Blake) Clap of Dorchester,

Mass., upon the eightieth anniversary of her birth presented to the First Church and Society in Warwick (her native town) $1,000; which was gratefully received by said Church and Society.

April 1, 1868, Mrs. Clap, on her eighty-fourth birthday, made to said Church and Society another donation of $1,000; which was received in the same spirit as the former.

July, 1868, Miss Mary Ann Hastings of Framingham, Mass., bequeathed to the First Society in Warwick the sum of $1,000, the income of which is to be for their use forever.

For this bequest a vote of thanks is entered on the Society's records.

THE CONGREGATIONAL CHURCH (ORTHODOX).

Rev. Roger C. Hatch, the second pastor of the Second Congregational Church in Warwick, after his dismission in 1853, resided in Warwick until the time of his death, which took place Sept. 12, 1868, at the advanced age of eighty years. During his residence here he was beloved and esteemed as a good citizen, a faithful pastor, an exemplary Christian, a true man, and devoted friend.

Since the dismission of Mr. Hatch, the church has been supplied by the Rev. Daniel C. Frost, Mr. Charles E. Bruce a licentiate from Northfield Academy, and others, until 1855, when Rev. Henry M. Bridge, formerly of the Methodist Church, was installed as its pastor. He was dismissed Dec. 20, 1859.

Rev. E. H. Blanchard was ordained over this

church April 25, 1860, and was dismissed May 11, 1868. Rev. Mr. Bissell supplied from June, 1868, for nearly a year. Rev. Edward Barnard Bassett was invited to preach Sept. 2, 1869; and he was installed as pastor Dec. 15, 1869, and is the present pastor of this church (1872).

We will here record an extract from "The Congregationalist and Boston Recorder" of Dec. 30, 1869: —

"The sermon at the installation of the Rev. Mr. Bassett over the church in Warwick was preached by the Rev. Dr. Barstow of Keene, N.H. Installing prayer by the Rev. H. B. Hooker, D.D. Charge to the pastor by the Rev. T. Cutler. Fellowship of the churches by Rev. A. B. Foster. Address to the people by Rev. E. Newton. Among the members of this little church, which is in the hill-country of Judæa, is a venerable mother in Israel, now in her ninety-second year. During thirteen years of her life, she read the Bible through every two months; and has read it through more than one hundred times in all. Now, near the shore of the better land, she realizes the value of the promise, 'And even to your old age I am He, and even to hoar hairs will I carry you.' And now we will introduce an incident of her early life, showing to the people of these railroad times how the people of Warwick travelled seventy years ago. This lady, Sarah Blake Leonard, then the wife of Francis Leonard, 2d, went to the residence of her father, Jonathan Blake, sen., in the following manner, — Mr. Leonard, his wife, and three children riding on one horse, and carrying from thirty to forty pounds of old iron in a bag; Mr. Leonard carrying a child on each arm, and his wife behind him carrying the baby in her lap, the iron swung across the saddle in the same way that the people of that day carried their grain to mill."

Congregational preachers originating from Warwick: Rev. John Fiske, D.D., Rev. Moses Fiske, Rev. Swan L. Pomroy, D.D., Rev. Nahum Gould, Rev. Junius L. Hatch, Rev. John Leonard, Rev. Francis Leonard, Rev. Levi Wheaton, Rev. George W. Barber. This society and church united in 1871, and painted and repaired their church edifice. They employed the Messrs. Graves to do the ornamental work; and they now have one of the neatest, the handsomest, and best-arranged churches, which is as ornamental and as well designed as any in this vicinity.

THE BAPTIST CHURCH IN WARWICK.

Exactly how early Baptists existed in this town we are not informed, but suppose that there were some as far back as 1797, when the church in Royalston was organized.

In the history of the West-Royalston church, written in 1854, we find the following: "In May, 1798, twenty-two members of this church signified their intention to form themselves into a church in Warwick; and they were dismissed agreeably to their request. At their first church-meeting, Elder Levi Hodge was chosen moderator."

As this church had come into being as the result of a difficulty, Elder Hodge acted the part of a peace maker: so much so, that, in 1801, the church in Royalston requested him to become their pastor; and Elder Hodge accepted of their invitation. In 1803, the two churches were united; and Mr. Hodge continued as its faithful pastor until the time of his death, in 1819, he all the time residing in Warwick. Elder J. M. Graves was the successor of Elder Hodge. In 1817, Elder John Shepardson purchased a farm in the south part of this town, and settled upon it. Here he lived until the day of his death, some time in 1833, and preached in the schoolhouse in the south part of Warwick, and in South Orange, and Erving's Grant, nearly every sabbath, working faithfully in the service of his *Master* to a good old age, when he was called to a better world on high, there to receive his reward.

On the 20th of January, 1843, fourteen persons, members of the Baptist church of Royalston and Warwick, petitioned to be set off as a branch of that church to meet in Warwick Centre. On the 14th of February following, the church voted to grant their request. The branch church chose Asa H. Conant clerk, and adjourned until April 1. At the adjourned meeting, Rev. E. M. Burnham was chosen pastor, and nine persons were added by letter from the South-Orange church, all of them inhabitants of Warwick.

An ecclesiastical council was convened Aug. 20, and organized by the choice of Rev. Asaph Meriam moderator, and Rev. Erastus Andrews clerk. The council voted to recognize them as an independent church. Mr. Burnham continued to labor as their pastor until Nov. 2, 1844, when he asked and obtained his dismission. Rev. L. Fay was then chosen pastor, and continued about two years. For the two following years, Rev. S. S. Kingsley was pastor. In 1849, Elder Fay again supplied the desk for about one year. Rev. Caleb Sawyer and others supplied the desk for nearly three years.

In 1854, Rev. E. M. Burnham labored with them for one-half of the time. The desk was supplied for the most part of 1856-1857 by Rev. Jonas G. Bennett. The report to the Association for 1858 was, "On the 1st of December last we parted with our late pastor, Rev. J. G. Bennett. The spring following (March), Rev. E. J. Emory came and filled the desk until April, 1861, when he received a call, and left for another part of his Master's vineyard."

In May, 1861, Rev. G. B. Bills became the pastor and remained for a little over a year. After he left, the church was without a pastor until autumn, when the Rev. Lyman Culver assumed the charge, and preached until the winter of 1863-64, when the desk was again supplied by the Rev. Erastus Andrews. From 1864 to 1868 the Rev. L. F. Shepardson was the pastor of this church. The Rev. L. Fay and others supplied the desk until June, 1869, after which the Rev. E. D. Daniels became pastor for one year; then the Rev. H. H. Woodbury supplied until the spring of 1871, when the Rev. C. Farrar became pastor, and continues to the present time. This church has received a donation of a thousand dollars the present year, from their deceased brother, Daniel Pierce, who gave to his brethren *in trust* for the *furtherance* of the *gospel* of *Christ*.

The following Baptist ministers originated from Warwick: Rev. Ebenezer Barber, Rev. Henry Holman, Rev. Jona. Blake.

UNIVERSALISTS.

The Universalist society in Warwick was incorporated Feb. 25, 1814, and has been supplied by Rev. Robert Bartlett, John Brooks, Stillman Clark, T. Barrow, E. Davis, and John H. Willis in 1851 and 1852, since which time they have had no regular preaching. They have no meeting-house.

The following Universalist ministers originated from Warwick: Rev. Caleb Rich, Robert Bartlett, Ebenezer Williams, and John Williams.

EPISCOPALIANS.

The Rev. Levi B. Stimson, an Episcopalian minister, originated from Warwick.

Summary of preachers who originated from Warwick: Orthodox Congregationalists, 9; Unitarians, 6; Universalists, 4; Baptists, 3; Episcopalian, 1, — making 23 different preachers as natives of this town.

SPIRITUALISM.

During the winter of 1850–51 quite a sensation was raised among the usually quiet people of our town by the announcement in the secular papers, that, in several places in this vicinity, what were at that time called the "Rochester knockings" were heard. But very little was known of the matter by the people of our town until March 5, 1851, when Mr. F. Cheney and wife of Athol came by invitation, and gave a public manifestation of the rappings, she being a medium for that phase of the phenomena. Quite a company having assembled, and being somewhat startled by what was heard, and the intelligence accompanying the sounds purporting to be communications from our departed friends that had left the mortal for the immortal shores, some of those present were favorably impressed on the subject, and returned home with a determination of giving the matter a further investigation. But little more was done until September following, when the tippings were to be seen at a number of places in this town, also exhibiting like intelligence. Early in October these manifestations became quite common at the house of Dea. Hervey Barber; and many were the visits that he and his family received from his townsmen, and from the people of the adjoining ones, who came to investigate these, at that time, new and almost miraculous movements. Soon after took place the phases of writing names and messages, and of seeing the forms of persons gone to the land of souls, who influenced one member of the family to speak and give information from the spirit world, and lectures on the reforms of the day, above the capacity of the individual that was used as the agent for the controlling power. These manifestations continued, and others were added to the list. One member of the family became clairvoyant, and another clairaudient; and nearly all the phases of mediumship now extant were there witnessed by large numbers: but they varied in their opinions as to the cause of the power that gave the intelligence they received. After considerable investigation, this family and several others became convinced that these demonstrations were what they claimed to be, — the testimony of our friends supposed to be dead ; that they still live, or, in other words, give a practical elucidation of the New-Testament doctrine of immortality. But as soon as it became known that it was claimed that these, or the like manifestations, were seen and heard at the time that Jesus and his apostles were upon the earth, and could be proved from the sacred Record, its believers, like those of old, "were everywhere spoken against;" and as the manifestations have continued with this family and several others, and as time has increased the number of the believers, and added strength to their faith in its divine origin and mission, and as the writer of this article is the only person in this town that has felt it to be his duty to preach this new gospel both at home and abroad, he and his associates desire that the above account of these things should be transmitted to posterity in this work, for their decision as to the utility and wisdom of their course.

THE GREAT HAIL-STORM.

On the 25th of July, 1866, a destructive storm of hail passed from north-west to south-east through the town, and extended into Orange.

After a very hot and sultry morning, some clouds were to be seen (not far from two o'clock, P.M.) near the western horizon : soon an unusual commotion was observed, both to the south-west and north-west, in the clouds, indicating severe storms of wind, rain, or hail. Both of these showers were attracted to a point near the western boundary of the town, called Notch Mountain. These storm-clouds met near the south side of said mountain; and near its southern base hail descended in large quantities, and the earth was covered to the depth of eight inches in this region. The hailstones were as large as walnuts, on an average: some of them were of the size of butternuts; and devastation and a general destruction of all vegetable matter was the consequence of the powers of the united storms. Not only were the crops of grain and fruit literally destroyed, but, for some distance each way on the south side of this mountain, the trees of the forest were so badly cut to pieces that nearly all of them died. Said storm passed from this place to the east, over the farms of Ezekiel Ellis; then to the south-east over those of Hervey Barber, C. W. Eddy, Henry M. Harvey, Albert Witherell, William H. Gale, and Ethan Cushing. These farms are located near the centre of its course: but the damage to the crops extended for more than a mile in width on each side; and all the crops, except grass, were entirely ruined. Many fowls were killed, and the roofs of many buildings so badly damaged as to oblige the owners to cover them anew, — the glass on one side, and some of them on two sides, was broken to fragments; and its path could be traced easily for several years afterwards.

It will be understood, that, on each side of the centre of the shower, the damage to the crops decreased as the distance increased; and, from its place of beginning to its end, the hailstones were continually becoming smaller, its fury abating, and the damage to crops less severe.

The citizens of Warwick that resided beneath its length and breadth were damaged to the amount of five thousand dollars, — perhaps more, as no true appraisal can be made; and no one storm of any kind, since the great tornado of 1821, has been the cause of the destruction of so large an amount of property. But our usually calm atmosphere and quiet earth were not left many days in peace; for, on the Saturday following, one of the heaviest showers of rain that was ever known fell on and about Mount Grace. For the space of over a mile, the rain actually *poured down for over an hour;* and the *mountain-rills* became *roaring torrents,* the *small brooks foaming rivers.* Many farms were injured to a large amount; and the highways that lead from the village towards Northfield and Winchester were in several places apparently ruined: so that the town was injured to a large amount in roads and bridges. Oct. 4, 1869, there was a general rain-storm in this vicinity. The rain fell for over six hours in torrents; and the destruction of property was greater than in 1866, as the storm extended over the whole town. The roads were damaged to a large amount. Many bridges were swept away: so that the public loss was considerable, but the private loss still greater. Among the sufferers were Martin Harris, David Shepardson, and James S. Wheeler, whose losses were great, and 'many others considerable. A few days after, there was quite a heavy shower in the north part of the town; and, as the ponds were already full, it broke A. I. Kidder's reservoir-dam, swept away his stave-mill, took down his saw-mill and dam, and left not a vestige of either to be seen upon the spot where they stood. It also broke several other dams, washing away bridges that came in the way; causing damage to over four thousand dollars within a very small distance.

April 25, 1872. — It being the ninety-fifth anniversary of the birth of Mr. Phinehas Child, his friends, to the number of thirty-six, assembled at the residence of his children, on Flower Hill in Warwick, and enjoyed a social season in a quiet way, by grasping the friendly hand, and conversing freely on the general subjects of the day, in which he still takes a lively interest, and calmly gives his opinion as in days gone by; for he retains his faculties, both mental and physical, in a remarkable degree for a man so far advanced in years. After partaking of a bountiful repast, furnished by the visitors, and listening to an explanation of an ornamental cake presented by the wife of the Rev. Charles Farrar, and an historic original poem written for the occasion, as a greeting of welcome for him to his friends, and expressing his thanks for their friendly call, the visitors departed to their homes, feeling that another milestone had been placed in their earthly path as well as in his, as a memento of love, respect, and kind regards to him for his long, useful, and honest life, and to themselves for their appreciation of virtue and moral worth in the character of one who has with several of them been a resident of our town for nearly sixty years.

INTRODUCTION TO THE APPENDIX

TO THE

HISTORY OF WARWICK.

We have thought it advisable, before giving the perusal of the Appendix to the History of Warwick, to present to our readers a brief genealogy of our deceased friend and fellow-citizen, the Hon. Jonathan Blake, and of his ancestors from the earliest settlement of New England, together with an account of his labors, and the responsible offices that he held, with specimens of his poems; believing it due to his descendants for what he did for our town during his long and useful life.   H. B.

[BY HIS BROTHER, SAMUEL BLAKE.]

Hon. Jonathan Blake was a descendant in the seventh generation from William and Agnes Blake of Dorchester, through Elder James, Dea. James, James "the annalist," Samuel, Jonathan. His ancestry is traced back four generations in England, prior to his emigrant ancestor, William, who was born in 1594.

Hon. Jonathan Blake, "the Historian of Warwick," was born in Dorchester, Mass., May 29, 1780.

He was son of Jonathan and Sarah (Pierce) Blake.*

His father moved to Warwick in 1781, and died there Oct. 8, 1836, in the eighty-eighth year of his age. His mother died Aug. 15, 1831.

Jonathan Blake married Patty Conant of Warwick, Jan. 18, 1803. They had six children.

She died in Warwick, Oct. 21, 1819.

He married, for his second wife, Mrs. Betsey (Howland) Ballard of Gill, Aug. 1, 1821.

He died April 13, 1864, at Brattleboro', Vt., aged eighty-four years.

He wrote the History of Warwick from its first settlement to the year 1854. He was a natural poet. He wrote a great amount of poetry on various subjects and on all occasions. He kept a voluminous diary for nearly sixty years.

He was in public business the most of his mature life. He was a distinguished surveyor of land, the practice of which profession has been peculiar to the Blake family from the first settlement of Massachusetts Bay. He was a friend to all public improvements, and an ardent advocate of railroads in their early days.

He resided in Warwick seventy-three (73) years.

Was town clerk of Warwick fifteen (15) years; served as selectman, overseer of the poor, and assessor nine (9) years; was acting justice of the peace forty-two (42) years; representative to the General Court two (2) years; senator of Massachusetts two (2) years; county commissioner in Franklin County nine (9) years, and chairman of the board three (3) years; a member of the Unitarian Church in Warwick over fifty years; superintendent of the sabbath school about twenty years. His influence was always

---

* See "Blake Family," page 56.

for good. He was a dutiful son, a beloved brother, a kind husband, a tender father, and has left posterity a rich patrimony in an example of an industrious, useful, and Christian life.

SPECIMENS OF THE POETRY OF HON. JONA. BLAKE.

WARWICK.

From Warwick's lofty mountains
    And everlasting hills
Flow many sparkling fountains,
    And precious, cooling rills.

How free from all diseases
    That mind and health impair!
How pure her summer breezes!
    How soft her balmy air!

Now, where in all creation
    Can such a place be found
For mental elevation
    To flourish and abound?

Proud Science here can flourish,
    And ever will prevail
To stimulate and nourish
    The mind that's sound and hale.

The votary of Pleasure
    Would here be sure to find
A more enduring treasure
    Than California's mine.

And Music's silvery tongues,
    In harmony divine,
Shall sing her glorious songs,
    Enchantingly sublime.

             And Wisdom's choicest treasures
                Shall raise her sons to fame,
             And bless their grand endeavors
                With an everlasting name.
                                              J. BLAKE.
BRATTLEBORO', Jan. 4, 1860.

SUNDAY-SCHOOL CELEBRATION.

IN QUESTIONS AND ANSWERS.

Ques. O KIND teachers! can you tell us
            Where the path to glory goes?
         Can you warn us of our dangers?
            Can you save us from our foes?

Ans.   Yes, dear children, we can tell you
            Of the road that leads to bliss:
         We can warn you of its dangers
            Through a world of sin like this.

Ques. O kind teachers! tell the story:
            How our bosoms pant to know
         What will make us good and happy
            While we live on earth below!

Ans.   Yes, dear children: 'tis the Bible, —
            Blessed book! — that tells the story, —
         How the young may love their Maker,
            How the saints prepare for glory.

Ques. O kind teachers! let us read it,
            Let us treasure up its meaning:
         All the good and great will love us;
            For 'twill make us leave off sinning.

Ans.   Blessed children, how we love you!
            We can never cease to praise
         Him who gave us all his bounty, —
            Life and health and peace and grace.
                                              J. BLAKE.
WARWICK, Oct. 2, 1841.

DEDICATION HYMN

FOR THE NEW UNITARIAN CHURCH IN WARWICK.

OMNIPOTENT and omniscient God,
Accept of this earthly abode
Our hands have upreared to thy name :
Let thy presence, like heavenly light,
Seraphic, diffusive, and bright,
Here come, and forever remain.

Let thy Spirit of peace, love, and joy,
Without any earthly alloy,
Descend like the dew that distils.
Harmonious and heavenly Guest,
Fill every worshipper's breast,
And soften our obdurate wills.

Inscribed on thy pages, O God!
Are words that thy goodness bestowed
To make us both happy and wise.
We hallow this temple to thee, —
The altar to which we would flee
To offer our best sacrifice.

We have built this house for thy praise :
Oh! make it a portal of grace
To usher us onward to heaven :
Like doves to their windows we'll come,
Or prodigals hastening home
To join in an endless thanksgiving.

J. BLAKE.

WARWICK, Oct. 4, 1836.

DEDICATION HYMN.

READ AT THE RE-DEDICATION OF THE UNITARIAN CHURCH, AFTER ITS REPAIRS.

To thee, our Maker and our God,
  We dedicate this house of prayer :
Here may we listen to thy word,
  And here thy benediction share !
Here may thy word like dew distil
  Its fragrance in this holy place,
And hearts submissive to thy will
  Its holy precepts to embrace !

Here may the strains from mortal tongues
  Begin the everlasting song, —
That endless, that eternal one,
  That, rapt in glory, saints prolong !
Here may the Spirit guide in prayer
  That erst descended from above,
And all our supplications share
  The blessing of redeeming love !

Here may our aged fathers come
  When on the tottering brink of time,
In earnest of that heavenly home,
  That better, holier, happier clime !
And here may all prepare to meet
  Their summons at our Saviour's call,
And, welcomed at his mercy-seat,
  The *great I Am!* the *All in All!*

J. BLAKE.

BRATTLEOBRO', July 3, 1859.

LINES TO BE SUNG AT A DONATION-PARTY IN WARWICK, MASS.

To Him that formed the starry skies
  Let all the praise be given, —
The Great, the Good, the Only Wise,
  Who sent his Son from heaven.

He came, a messenger of peace,
  Glad tidings to proclaim,
Of endless joys and happiness, —
  All in his Father's name.

He told us where our duty lies;
  How love to God is shown —
Better than formal sacrifice —
  By *love* to every *one*.

Our harps upon the willows hung,
  Like captive Jews of old;
God's house shut up, his praise unsung,
  No one to pen the fold.

In kindness and in love appears
  A friend in time of need,
Whose generous heart dispels our fears,
  And sows the precious seed.

We meet this day to consecrate,
  Each one, their little mite
To him whose labors here of late
  Proclaim what's good and right.

God grant him peace and happiness,
  And we'll reward his care;
And may his work of righteousness
  Each one for heaven prepare!

J. BLAKE.

BRATTLEBORO', Nov. 12, 1858.

LINES OF CONDOLENCE

ADDRESSED TO MR. AND MRS. ———, ON THE DEATH OF THEIR DAUGHTER.

PARENTAL love may strive to save
A blooming infant from the grave, —
   The object of their love;
But purer love and higher claims
The God who made it still maintains,
   And summoned it above.

Sweet little child, it dies, it dies!
Its breath departs, its spirit flies,
   And leaves its clog of dust;
While shining seraphs guide it home,
Up to its heavenly Father's throne,
   To dwell among the just.

In faith convey its body on,
Commit its keeping to the tomb:
   It cannot there remain.
(A grain of wheat must die to grow
In richest soil where waters flow)
   Your child shall live again.

Though sown a mortal, sure she'll rise
Immortal heir of paradise,
   Of purity and bliss;
And, clothed in garments white and clean,
Forever praise thee, One supreme,
   In endless happiness.

                              J. BLAKE.

DORCHESTER, Oct. 25, 1851.

APPENDIX

TO THE HISTORY OF WARWICK.

WE now come to the second part of our work, which we entitle an Appendix to the History of Warwick, wherein we record some incidents not mentioned in Mr. Blake's manuscript; and, not wishing to interfere with his arrangements, we place them in this part, so that they may be kept for the benefit of future generations. With some of those that he has recorded, we have added such further explanations as we thought needful to make them well understood, and others not so much of direct history as those in the first part of our volume; but we think they will be of interest to some families, as their ancestors were the principal actors in the events here recorded.

We will here insert the names of the owners of the fifty-acre or home lots, when surveyed in 1737; also, who owned the same lots when the first plan of the township of Gardner's Canada (now Warwick) was made; who owned, or were settled on said lots in 1761, when all the settlers' names were taken at the new meeting-house in said town, by order of the proprietors; and also who reside on or own these lots at the present time, 1872, as near as we can determine by the proprietors' plan, containing a survey of the said lots, and the one hundred acre-lots surveyed in 1738:—

No.	Owners in 1737.	A few years after.	1761	1872
1	Samuel Stevens	Samuel Stevens	not settled	B. Davis's place
2	Benj. Smith	Benj. Smith	Geo. Robbins	A. Blake, mills
3	Gresham Davis	G. Davis	not settled	E. Collar's place
4	Wm. Dudley	Wm. Dudley	John Goodale	Morris Coughlin, pasture
5	Jos. Weld	Jos. Weld	Moses Evans	Coughlin and J. Blake
6	Jos. Gardner	Jos. Heath	not settled	Coughlin & others (in part)
7	Eleazer Hammond	E. Hammond	not settled	J. Shepardson (in part)
8	Josiah Cheney	J. Cheney	not settled	I. Whittimore's heirs
9	Peter Aspinwall	P. Aspinwall	Sam'l Pratt	Whitmore and Flagg (in part)
10	John Wilson	Benj. Wilson	not settled	J. Leonard, farm
11	Wm. Sharp	Wm Sharp	Sam'l Ball	J. W. Green, farm
12	Ebnr. Smith	Elias Smith	Mosely Alvard	W. Flagg (in part)
13	Sam'l Griffin	Sam'l Griffin	not settled	W. Flagg and others
14	Ebnr. Case	Elias Clark	Amariah Roberts	R. Knight, farm
15	Sam'l Newall	James Ball	not settled	Bird's pasture. &c.
16	Edward White	E. White	John Brandon	W. Burnett, farm
17	Sam'l Fisher	Sam'l Tucker	Tim. Nurse	W. B. farm, and Coughlin, north part
18	Ebnr. Crafts	Stephen Wall	not settled	Green and Moore
19	Sam'l Peacock	Ira Welch	" "	Kimball & others
20	John Parker	John Foster	Joseph Perry	Kimball & others
21	Joseph Heath	Joseph Waite	Ichabod Johnson	Patridge & others
22	Sam'l Wight	Sam'l Wight	not settled	N. Jones & others
23	Joseph Weld	Joseph Weld	Andrew Blunt	D. N. Shepardson
24	Isaac Stedman	Isaiah Allen	Amos Marsh	Houghton place
25	Samuel Davis	Sam'l Davis	not settled	H. Williams
26	Samuel Clark	Sam'l Clark	Nathan Stevens	John Morse
27	E. Hammond	E. Hammond	David Bassett	E. Barber, pasture
28	John Shepard	Joseph Shepard	not settled	A. Albee's, Cook place
29	Thos. Hartshorn	Thos. Hartshorn	" "	Fisk Cemetery, &c., Fisk place
30	John Gay	John Seaver	Ebnr. Davis	Barnard Fisher
31	Minister lot	Minister lot	not settled	H. M Harvey
32	Ministry lot	Ministry lot	" "	Wid. Holbrook
33	Edward Morris	Edward Morris	Israel Olmstead	C. W Hastings
34	Ebnr. Crafts	Ebenr. Cragin	Simeon Olmstead	S. Reed, Smith place
35	Ebnr. Maude	E. Maurice	Sam'l Scott	Sam'l Reed
36	James Frizzell	J. Frizzell	Sam'l Spaulding	James Goldsbury
37	Joseph Heath	Jos. Heath	Amzi Doolittle Jos Mayo	J. Goldsbury and others
38	Thomas Mayo	Thomas Mayo	A. Doolittle, jun.	Elisha Brown
39	John Seaver	John Seaver	Sam'l Scott, jun.	E. Brown & others
40	Israel Hearsay	Sam'l Morse	Sam'l Bennett	W. E. Russell's pasture

APPENDIX. 185

No	Owners in 1737.	A few years after.	1761.	1872.
41	Benj. White	Gershom Davis	Moses Evans	M M Stevens
42	Wm. Dudley	Joseph Gould	Moses Evans	M. M. Stevens & others
43	Wm Dudley	Charles Marsh	Moses Evans	A. K Litchfield
44	Robert Harris	Robert Harris	James Ball	Litchfield and Goldsbury
45	John Masecroft	Wm. Dudley	Thomas Rich	Cassius Goldsbury
46	Benj. Bugbee	Wm. Dudley	Jonathan Perry	J. & J. Goldsbury
47	Joseph Daniels	Robert Harris	Joseph Goodale	Joseph Pierce
48	John Chandler	Jno. Chandler	David Allen	G. H. Richards
49	Timothy Mosman	Timo. Mosman	Edward Allen	E. & E. F. Mayo
50	Sam'l Perry	Sam'l Perry	Barnabas Russell	Messrs. Mayo and others
51	Timothy Whitney	Timo. Whitney	Nathan Ball	Messrs. Mayo and others, Ball Farm
52	Robert Sharp	Robert Sharp	Moses Leonard	Messrs. Mayo and others, Ball Farm
53	John Allen	John Mayo	David Ayers	Asa Gould and others
54	Shubael Seaver	Joseph Weeks	David Ayers, jun.	Heirs of D. Tyler
55	Thomas Taft	Robert Daniels	not settled	Heirs of D. Tyler
56	Andrew Gardner	Robert Heath	Jedediah Wood	C. G. A. Prentice
57	Robert Daniels	Robert Bennett	Abner Coffin	C. Hastings
58	Thomas Mayo	Thos. Mayo	Silas Town	John Stearns
59	Andrew Seaver	A. Seaver	not settled	John Stearns
60	John Ruggles	John Ruggles	" "	J. Stearns and others
61	John Parker	John Parker	Charles Woods	John Whipple
62	John Willson	John Willson	E. Prestcott	R. Weeks's heirs
63	School lot	School lot	not settled	Wid Lois Smith

THE WAR OF 1812–14.

This war with Great Britain was declared by a vote of the Congress of the United States, in the month of June, 1812, by a vote of seventy-nine to forty-nine in the House, and of nineteen to thirteen in the Senate; and, on the 18th, Pres. Madison signed the bill, and war was formally declared the next day. In this war the citizens of Warwick took an active part in defence of their country's rights, although a majority of them were opposed to its declaration. Among those that enlisted in the United-States service were John Ager, George Stockwell, Henry Whipple, and —— Parmenter (privates); Benjamin Eddy (drum-major); Obadiah Bass (musician).

We find on the records of the South company of the Militia in our town the following regimental orders : —

To Capt. William Burnett, Jun.

In pursuance of Brigade Orders, bearing date of Sept. 9, 1814, you are hereby commanded to detach forthwith, from the company under your command, one ensign, one sergeant, and fourteen privates, well armed and equipped, as the law directs. You are likewise further commanded to parade your detached men near the academy, in New Salem, on Tuesday the thirteenth day of September, inst., at nine o'clock, A.M., and there to wait for further orders.

BENJ. S. WELLS,
Col. 3d Regt., 2d Brig., 4th Div.

MONTAGUE, Sept. 9, 1814.

SEPT. 11, 1814.

Agreeable to regimental orders, a training was appointed to be held on Monday, Sept. 12, 1814; and the clerk received orders from Capt. Wm. Burnett for warning the company, which was duly performed according to orders.

SEPT. 12, 1814.

Agreeable to appointment and legal notice, the company met at the usual place of parade at eight o'clock, A.M., and was called to order by the captain. Voted and chose Cummins Lesure clerk *pro tem*. The company roll was called, and other duty performed; and a detachment was made, and the following persons were detached ; viz., Ebenezer Stearns (ensign); Ebenezer Barber (sergeant); Ephraim Tuel, Manning Wheelock, Jonas Leonard, Willard Packard, Dexter Fisk, David Gale, Jun., Stephen Ball, William Boyle, Abijah Eddy, Jonas Conant, Samuel Abbot, Peter Warrick, Daniel Smith, Artemas Baker (privates).

(Attest)   LEMUEL WHEELOCK, *Clerk*.

The above order was also issued to the North company in town; and said company was called together accordingly. But, as the records of said company have not been found, we therefore add the following names of persons, that, as we are informed, were detached on said occasion for like services: Abner Goodale (ensign); Nathan Atwood, Stephen Williams, Joseph Williams, jun., James Ball, jun., Samuel Ball, Ezra Ripley, Eli Stockwell, —— Maxwell (privates).

Stephen Gale, Benoni Ballou, George Jaseph, Joseph Jaseph, James Fuller, and some others, went into the service in place of some of the detached men, they having been hired in their stead. Of the aforesaid only these are now living in Warwick: Ebenezer Barber, Henry Whipple.

During the autumn of 1814, John Quincy Adams and others, from the government of the United States, were sent to Ghent, in Belgium, to meet commissioners from Great Britain; and, on the 24th of December, a treaty of peace was signed. The news reached our country Feb. 11, 1815. Late at night a horseman was heard galloping through the streets of Washington with news of peace; and "Peace! peace!" soon resounded on all sides.

The joyful news soon circulated throughout the country. It was here, when received, as well as everywhere else, hailed with delight which would, at this time of railroads, steamboats, and telegraph wires, be considered tardy in the extreme. And on the eighteenth day of February, the treaty was ratified by the United-States Senate; and peace was thereby secured, leaving a government debt of over a hundred million dollars, with our commerce destroyed, and all kinds of industry depressed. But we are proud to affirm, that, under the influence of our free institutions, the above debt was in a few years all paid, and a large amount of surplus revenue divided among the States.

An Extract from the Reflections on the Tornado which passed from Northfield, through Warwick, to Orange, Sept. 9, 1821. By Elder John Shepardson, Warwick, January, 1822.

    How mighty is the voice of God!
        How heavy is his hand!
    When once he sways his awful rod,
        None can his power withstand.
    Oft has he spoke, of ancient date,
        As many writers say;
    And now he speaks to us of late
        In a surprising way.

    From western sky a cloud arose,
        Some thunder and some rain;
    A wind which nothing could oppose, —
        It swept both hill and plain.
    It broke the trees of largest size,
        Tore up the flinty rocks,
    Striking all nature with surprise,
        Disturbed the peaceful flocks.

    It swept off barns, and houses too,
        With all the goods they owned,
    Leaving whole families in woe,
        And some with broken bones.
    But oh! the most surprising stroke,
        Too shocking to relate:
    Two blooming youths by whirlwind spoke
        To the eternal state.

    Oh! come, ye living, search and spy,
        And view the wonder well;
    Go forth from Northfield mountain high
        To Orange lofty hill;
    Go see the wounded, hear their groans,
        And hear the mourner's cries;
    See the rent earth her God doth own
        With wonder and surprise.

APPENDIX.

We will here insert, for the purpose of preserving them, the names of our truly noble sons who toiled, bled, suffered, and died in the service of their country during the war of the Rebellion.

Some of them removed from town prior to the commencement of the war, but had not become residents of any other place previous to their enlistment into the Union army. All honor to such!

We will first record the names of those that died; and their names are inscribed on our Soldiers' Monument: —

Henry W. Lawrence,	James D. Delvee,	Leander S. Jillson,
Francis L. Moore,	Charles Jones,	M. Stanley Cushing,
Levi E. Switzer,	Jas. Henry Fuller,	Monroe L. B. Patridge,
Frederic Williams,	Willard Packard,	Joseph Drake,
Benjamin Hastings,	Franklin Pierce,	Edwards Davis,
LaFayette Nelson,	John B. Caldwell,	James M. Chapin,
Edward N. Coller,	Warren H. Blake,	Jacob S. Rayner, jun.,
Seth A. Woodward,	Joseph W. Sawyer,	S. P. Shepardson, jun.,
Henry H. Manning,	Alexander Cooper,	Joseph W. Ellis (27).

The following are the names of those that returned, and are now residing in Warwick: —

Lyman Mason,	Rayal E. Stimson,	Harwood S. Proctor,
Nath. M. Pond,	Jesse F. Bridge,	Joseph A. Williams,
Henry H. Jillson,	George Jennings,	William Dugan (11).
Dwight S. Jennings,	George E. Cook,	

Names of those that returned, but removed to other places: —

Joseph Spencer,	Richards Mayo,	Charles Lawrence,
Henry O. Cook,	Henry Witherell,	Theodore Putnam,
George Mason,	Alonzo Scott,	Jairus Hammond,
Frederic Quinn,	Dwight E. Stone,	Albert C. Barber,
Amory Gould, 2d,	Orrin Curtis,	Artemus W. Ward.
Alphonzo Rayner,	Chas. E. Randall,	Richard Weeks, jun.,

William Weeks,	Sumner Lincoln,	Amos Taylor, 3d,
Francis L. Fuller,	Peter Dyer,	Alfred Houghton,
Joseph Putnam,	John Farnsworth,	Elliot Stone,
R. Harding Barber,	Lewis Atwood,	Charles W. Higgins,
Henry W. Kidder,	William H. Mason,	Albert L. Hunt,
Andrew J. Curtis,	A. R. Jennings,	Silas Jennings,
George Severance,	Joseph Adams,	Samuel Adams,
George B. Cobb,	S. T. Underwood,	*Total*, 41

Joseph Draper and Luke Delvee were drafted and accepted, and each procured a substitute.

Charles Goldsbury, William H. Gale, M. W. S. Clark, *Henry O. Cook, *Dwight S. Jennings, Josiah Conant, 2d, George A. Cushing, and John M. Putney, were also drafted and accepted, and paid three hundred dollars each themselves, or by their friends, and substitutes procured by the selectmen, or others. Total, eight. In all lists, seventy-nine.

THE REBEL BELL.

WE'VE got a bell from Rebeldom, —
  A secesh bell, I mean, —
Suspended from our school-house dome,
  Upon the village green.

Its voice rings out at morn and noon
  To call the happy throng
Away from sports and games,
  From mirth and laugh and song.

We know not where it used to hang,
  Nor whom it used to call:
If amid scenes of mirth or grief
  Its notes were wont to fall.

---

* Drafted after discharged and returned from the army

The rebels had designed to send
　　This bell to Yankee foes, —
Not all at once to ring for school,
　　But how, the soldier knows.

Perhaps its hanging here will save
　　The life of some soldier brave;
And he'll come back to friends and home, —
　　Not fill a soldier's grave.

We will not call it rebel now,
　　Here in this North land free:
It shall not stay and do its work,
　　And still a rebel be.

Oh, no! a rebel at the North
　　Is what we all despise;
Then we'll rechristen and rename
　　Our little rebel prize.

And let it hang and do its work;
　　And, when the war shall end,
It shall ring out with joyful shout, —
　　Its voice with others blend,

To welcome back our soldier band,
　　Our soldiers true and brave,
Who are fighting, 'neath a Southern sky,
　　For the Union and the slave.

Then let it ring at morn and noon,
　　No more a *rebel bell:*
Its voice shall teach us liberty,
　　It freedom's words shall tell.

And may all those who enter here,
　　Or listen to its voice,
Make *wisdom*, knowledge, liberty,
　　Their earnest, lasting choice.

　　　　　　　　　　　　SUSIE E. BARBER.

WARWICK, Dec. 20, 1862.

Said bell was taken from the rebels at New Orleans, on its way to the foundry to be cast into shot and shell to be sent by ordnance into the Union army; which incited the author to compose the above lines, which were read on that occasion.

LIST OF TOWN OFFICERS, &c.

[WRITTEN BY J. BLAKE IN 1832.]

There have been thirteen physicians established in this town for a longer or shorter term of time, only two of whom have died here. Their names are, —

Medad Pomeroy, Benjamin Hazeltine, John Garfield, Ezra Conant, jun., ——— Fairfield, ——— Bliss, John Willson, Peletiah Metcalf, Ebenezer Hall, Ebenezer Chaplin, Artemas Baker, Joel Burnett, and Amos Taylor.

There has never been but one lawyer who attempted to gain a living among us; viz., Henry Barnard, Esq.

There have been fourteen different persons chosen representatives to the General Court; viz.: —

	No. years' service.		No. years' service.
Deacon James Ball	2	Dea. Caleb Mayo	7
Col. Samuel Williams	2	Ebenezer Williams	1
Thomas Rich	3	Justus Russell	3
John Goldsbury	9	Jonathan Blake, jun.	2
Nathaniel Cheney	1	Joseph Stevens	3
Oliver Chapin	3	Lemuel Wheelock	1
Josiah Cobb	8	Ashbel Ward	2

· We have been represented forty-seven years, and have been without a representative twenty-two years, since the town was incorporated. There have been twelve town clerks, who served the number of years set against their names, —

APPENDIX. 193

	No. years' service.		No. years' service.
Dea. James Ball	12	Josiah Pomeroy, jun.	12
Amos Marsh	4	Jonathan Blake, jun.	15
Col. Samuel Williams	3	Ebenezer Hall	4
Ezra Conant	9	William Cobb, jun.	1
Dr. Ezra Conant, jun.	1	Asa Thayer	1
John Conant	9	Dr. Amos Taylor	3

ALL THE SELECTMEN, SINCE THE TOWN WAS INCORPORATED, AND THE NUMBER OF YEARS THEY SERVED SET AGAINST THEIR NAMES.

	Year.		Year.
Moses Evans	1	John Whitney	1
Jonathan Woodard	1	Jacob Estey	1
David Buckman	1	Zachariah Barber	1
John Ormsbee	1	Ebenezer Pierce	1
Peter Procter	1	Perez Allen	1
Daniel Whitney	1	Elias Knowlton	1
Ebenezer Cheney	1	William Burnett, jun.	1
Jacob Rich	1	Elijah Fisk	1
Joel Pierce	1	Jacob R. Gale	1
Reuben Shattuck	1	Josiah Rawson	1

Making twenty selectmen that served one year each.

Here follow those that have served two years:—

	Years.		Years.
Joseph Gilbert	2	Nathaniel Rich	2
Ezra Conant	2	William Cobb	2
David Cobb	2	Abijah Eddy	2
Seth Peck	2	Ansel Lesure	2
Joseph Mayo	2	Samuel Ball	2

Making ten that have served two years each.

Those that served three years:—

	Years.		Years.
Amzi Doolittle	3	Ebenezer Stearns	3
Col. Samuel Williams	3	Ebenezer Barber	3
Samuel Langley	3	Col. James Goldsbury	3
Dr. John Willson	3	Total seven.	

Those that served four years: —

	Years.		Years.
Josiah Pomeroy	4	Amory Gale	4
Josiah Procter	4	Total, three.	

Those that served five years: —

	Years.		Years.
Benjamin Conant	5	Joseph Stevens	5
Benjamin Simonds	5	Total, four.	
Capt. John Goldsbury	5		

Those that served six years: —

	Years.		Years.
Nathaniel G. Stevens	6	Justus Russell	6
		Total, two.	

Those that served seven years: —

	Years.		Years.
Jeduthan Morse	7	Ebenezer Williams	7
Thomas Rich	7	Lemuel Wheelock	7
Jonathan Gale	7	Total, five.	

Only one that served eight years, —

    Dr. Medad Pomeroy, eight years.

Those that served nine years: —

	Years.		Years.
Jonathan Blake, Jr.	9	Caleb Mayo	9
Amos Marsh	9	Joshua Atwood	9
Mark Moore	9	Total, five.	

Those that served ten years: —

	Years.		Years.
Dea. James Ball	10	Ashbel Ward	10
		Total, two.	

Only one person served eleven years, — Col. James Goldsbury . 11
Only one person served sixteen years, — Josiah Cobb . . 16

Making sixty-one different selectmen; and nearly one-third of them served only one year each.

The above account is from the incorporation of the town up to and including the year 1832.

[WRITTEN BY J. BLAKE IN 1854.]

In the past twenty-two years, we have chosen nine different persons for representatives to the General Court. (Lemuel Wheelock had served one year before 1832), making twenty-two different persons that have represented this town since it was incorporated.

Clark Stearns served one year,	1	Making three persons that have served one year since 1832, and add two before, making five in all that served one year, 5
Ansel Davis " "	1	
Samuel W. Spooner served one year,	1	
	3	

Those that served two years : —

William E. Russell,	2 years	These three add to four that served before 1832, making seven in all that served two years, 7
Ira Draper,	2 "	
John G. Gale,	2 "	
	3	

Served three years : —

Jacob C. Gale,	3 years	Add these two to four that served before 1832, making six in all for for three years, 6
Abijah Eddy,	3 "	
	2	

Served six years : —

Lemuel Wheelock, by adding one year before 1832 . . . 1
Caleb Mayo, served seven years before 1832 1
Josiah Cobb, served eight years before 1832 1
John Goldsbury served nine years before 1832 . . . 1

Twenty-two different representatives.   22

The town has been represented sixty-seven years since it was incorporated, ninety-one years ago, and has been unrepresented twenty-four years.

Jonathan Blake, jun., was chosen a delegate to the convention for amending the Constitution of the State in 1820.

Samuel W. Spooner was chosen a delegate to the convention for amending the Constitution in 1853.

I have never seen any record of there being a delegate in the convention from this town, when our State Constitution was adopted in 1780.

Town clerks, with the number of years they held the office, since 1832 : —

Amos Taylor,	6 years	There had been twelve different persons before 1832, and four since that time. Amos Taylor had served three years before and six years since, making nine years in all. So there have been sixteen town clerks, all told.
Lemuel Wheelock,	2 "	
Abijah Eddy,	6 "	
George Chesebro,	3 "	
Ira Draper,	5 "	

All the selectmen that had held that office before 1832 were sixty-one. Since 1832 we have had eighteen different persons.

Served one year : —

Joel Pierce,	1 year	Add these two to twenty previous ones, makes 22 that served one year only ; Ibri Baker, chosen this year, call	22
Harvey Conant,	1 "		
	—		
	2		1

Those that served two years : —

Asa Wheeler, two years, added to ten previous ones, makes		.	11
S. N. Atwood,	2 years	And both chosen this year, which 3 shall add with those that have before.	
Edward F. Mayo,	2 "		

APPENDIX.

Served three years: —

Samuel Blake,	3 years	
David Gale, jun.	3 "	
David Burnett,	3 "	Added to 7 that served before
Clark Stearns,	3 "	1832, making a total of 15
George W. Moore,	3 ."	that served three years each, 15
John G. Gale,	3 "	
	—	
	8	

Those that served four years: —

William E. Russell,	4 years	
James Stockwell,	4 "	Added to three that served pre-
Hervey Barber,	4 "	vious to 1832, total, 6
	—	
	3	

Those selectmen that served five years: —

Jasper Leland,	5 years	
Ira Draper,	5 "	Added to four that served pre-
	—	vious to 1832, makes total, 6
	2	

Those that served six years: —

Joseph Stevens, three, added to } Which, with two others before
three before, 6 years } 1832, make 3

Those that served seven years: —

Jacob R. Gale, six years since } One, added to five previous
1832, and one before, makes 7; } ones, makes 6

Dr. Medad Pomeroy served eight years previous to 1832   1
Five different persons served nine years each previous to 1832 .   5
Two   "   "   "   ten years each   "   "   .   2
One   "   "   "   eleven years   "   "   .   1
One   "   "   "   sixteen years   "   "   .   1
                                                              80

Making eighty different selectmen since the town was incorporated, and the number of years each has served.

RESIDENTS OF WARWICK OVER SEVENTY YEARS OF AGE.

Names of the Males.	Age.	Names of the Females.	Age.
Asa Atwood (pauper)	70	Mary Lincoln	79
Cushing Lincoln	79	Lucinda Gale (widow)	78
Phinehas Child (widower)	76	Lois Goddard (widow)	84
Justus Russell	77	Esther Morton (wid., pauper)	78
Stephen Johnson (pauper)	75	Azubah Whitmore (pauper)	75
Josiah Conant (widower)	90	Elizabeth Whipple (widow)	71
Nathan C. Morse	79	Sarah Leonard (widow)	75
Jonas Conant	78	Martha Leonard (widow)	80
Benjamin Conant	78	Eunice Morse	70
Simeon Stearns	74	Hannah Lesure (w., pensioner)	90
David Ball	73	Eunice Stearns (single)	83
Asa Bancroft	73	Tamer Stearns (single)	71
Caleb Weeks	78	Sarah Penniman (widow)	77
Joseph Draper (widower)	80	Mary Gale (widow)	83
Ezekiel Nelson	78	Sophia Whitney (single)	74
Daniel Whitmore (pauper)	80	Polly Davis	74
Aaron Bass	71	Polly Johnson	71
Samuel Williams (widower)	73	Betsey Conant	72
Isaac Hastings	71	Susannah Blake (widow)	70
Elijah Davis	82	Lucy Eddy (single)	71
William Howard	76	Sally Weeks	75
Luther Smith	71	Polly Knowlton (widow)	74
Amos K. Whitney (widower)	79	Lucy Field (single)	74
John Stearns	73	Eunice Barnard (w., pauper)	80
Erastus Morgan (pensioner)	89	Anne Conant	71
Jonathan Blake	73	Leafy Howard	75
		Rose Sandin (widow)	70
Males	26	Amy Kelton (widow)	70
Females	33	Elizabeth Spencer (widow)	70
		Rebecca Brown (widow)	81
Total over seventy years.	59	Lydia Stockwell (widow)	70
on Feb. 1, 1854, at which time the above was taken.		Hannah Leland (widow)	80
		Sally Mallory (single)	70
			33

There are now two persons in town over ninety years of

age, — one man and one woman; eleven between eighty and ninety years of age, — four men and seven women; and forty-six between the age of seventy and eighty years. Of the above, five are widowers, and eighteen are widows; six are maiden ladies. There are two pensioners, — one man and one woman. Six of the above are maintained by the town; viz., three men and three women.

There is but one doctor to add to the thirteen that we counted in 1832, and he was here but a few years, and then removed to Montague; viz., Dr. George Wright. Dr. Amos Taylor, before mentioned, is the one now practising here, and has been the principal physician for nearly forty years. The first and only postmaster we have had until within a year was William Cobb, who held that office nearly fifty years, and until his death.

[WRITTEN BY DEACON HERVEY BARBER, 1872.]

The whole number of persons chosen by the town, previous to 1854, to represent them in the Legislature of the Commonwealth, was twenty-two. In 1855 and 1856, the town voted not to send. Since that time our town has been incorporated into a district with Orange and New Salem for that purpose. Said district has been represented by a citizen of Warwick four times since its incorporation, by three different persons; viz., Nathaniel E. Stevens, Esq., one year; Rev. I. S. Lincoln, two years; and E. F. Mayo, Esq., one year. The remainder of the time the district has been represented by citizens of Orange and New Salem.

Previous to 1854, eighty different persons had been chosen, and served as selectmen of the town; and the names and the years each one has served are to be found in the former pages of this work.

From 1854 to 1872, inclusive, seventeen persons have performed like duties; viz., James L. Stockwell, one year;

and Ibri Baker, Clark Stearns, N. E. Stevens, S. W. Jillson, Hervey Barber, Eben G. Ball, for two years each.

Henry G. Mallard, Charles R. Gale, William H. Gale, Lyman Atwood, for the term of three years each.

S. N. Atwood, William H. Bass, Jesse F. Bridge, each for four years; and Edward F. Mayo for the space of nine years, he having served three years prior to that time, making twelve years in all. S. N. Atwood had also served three years previous, making seven in all. Hervey Barber, four previous, making six years as his time of service. Clark Stearns, three before; showing that he has served five years. Ibri Baker, one prior, two subsequent, making three for him : so that we can now add twelve more names to the honorable list that has preceded, namely, eighty ; it being a sum total of ninety-two citizens of our town that have been elected as selectmen, and performed the onerous duties of that important office, since we have been known as the town of Warwick, — a little over a hundred and nine years. For twenty-seven years previous to 1763, under the proprietors, we were known as Gardner's Canada ; and from time immemorial prior to 1736, "This country, that surrounds our beautiful Mount Grace, was called Sheomet, its Indian name."

In summing up the above statement, we find that the persons that have served one year as selectmen are 23 ; those that have served two years, 14 ; also those that have served three years, 17 ; and those that served for four years, 9 ; also for five years, 8 ; and for six years, 3 ; for seven years, 7 ; for eight years, 1 ; for nine years, 5 ; for ten years, 2 ; for eleven years, 1 ; for twelve years, 1 ; for sixteen years, 1 : making a total of 92 in all, since 1763.

The town first elected a superintending school-committee at the annual March meeting, 1814. Before that time, the resident clergyman performed that service, it being considered a part of his parochial duties ; and from 1814 to

1827, inclusive, Rev. Preserved Smith served as an honorary member and chairman of the Board; and from 1822 to 1825 the town neglected to choose any school-committee, as there are no names found upon the town records for that responsible office: so the Rev. P. Smith ably and satisfactorily performed all the labor of that very important station for that term of years. In 1826, the town, at Mr. Smith's request, elected Dea. Josiah Proctor, Dr. Amos Taylor, and Capt. Ebenezer Barber, to assist him in its onerous duties. And from that time to the present, 1872, the town has annually chosen from three to twelve persons to serve them in that capacity.

From that time, 1814, to the present, the following persons have been elected, and have served the town in the capacity of Superintending School Committee, for the following terms of years, including 1832: —

Joshua Atwood,	Dea. Caleb Mayo,	John Whitney, jun.,
Manning Wheelock,	Thomas White, jun.,	Dea. Joel Pierce,
Calvin Allen,	Dea. G. W. Moore,	Dea. Edward Mayo,
Cushing Lincoln,	Jasper Leland,	Thomas Chase, jun.,
Dea. John Leonard,	Joshua Williams, jun,	George Jones,
Rev. D. H. Barlow,	A. C. Felton,	Harvey Conant,
Otis Brooks, Esq.,	H. G. Mallard, Esq.,	Rev. A. Jackson,
James Goldsbury, jun.,	James Stockwell, Esq.,	Lyman Rich,
Dr. C. J. Barber,	Harry Grout,	Chandler W. Bass,
E. S. Proctor,	Luke Delvee,	George A. Cushing.

Thirty persons, in all, that have served one year.

Eben'r Williams, Esq.,	Amos K. Whitney,	James Kelton, jun.,
Capt. John Stearns,	Samuel Moses, jun.,	Harvey Robbins,
Rev. S. S. Kingsley,	Rev. George F. Clark,	George N. Richards,
Dea. D. Tyler,	George W. Smith,	Rev. W. A. P. Willard,
D. M. Shepardson,	William H. Bass,	Rev. John Shephardson.

Fifteen persons that have served two years.

Dr. Ebenezer Hall,   Dea. Ebenezer Pierce, Joseph Stephens, Esq.,
Rev. Sam'l Kingsbury, Chas. Pomeroy, Esq., Benj. R. Felton, Esq.,
Rev. H. M. Bridge,   Gilman Brown,   Albert Witherell,
James L. Stockwell, William H. Gale,   Joseph Clark.

Twelve persons for three years.

Capt. Ebenezer Barber,   James Goldsbury, Esq.,
Dr. George Wright,   Wm. E. Russell, Esq.

Four persons for four years.

Clark Stearns, Esq.,   Martin Harris,   Appleton Gale,
Justus Russell, Esq., Abijah Eddy, Esq.,   E. F. Mayo, Esq.,
                       Rev. John Goldsbury.

Seven persons for five years.

Charles R. Gale,   Eben G. Ball, Esq.,   Henry K. Atwood.

Three persons for six years.

Col. B. G. Putnam,   John Stearns, jun.,   J. A. J. Moore,
James S. Wheeler,   Lem'l Wheelock, Esq.,   Jona. Blake, Esq.
                     Dr. Amos Taylor,

Seven persons for seven years.

Rev. Roger C. Hatch, one for nine years.
Dr. Gardner C. Hill, one for ten years.
Rev. Preserved Smith, one for sixteen years.
Dea. Hervey Barber, one for eighteen years.

Making eighty-two persons that have served in that responsible office in fifty-four years.

The number of persons that had served as town clerk prior to 1854 was sixteen. Since that time, Ira Draper has been town-clerk five years, Henry G. Mallard one year, Edward F. Mayo seven years, and A. S. Atherton five years, including the present. Ira Draper had served five years previous ; making nineteen persons in all that have served since the incorporation of the town.

From the year 1802 to the present (1872), William Cobb, Esq., was chosen, and acted as town treasurer forty-seven years ; James Goldsbury, Esq., nine ; Rev. R. C. Hatch, one ; Col. B. G. Putnam, four ; Phillip Young, four ; and A. S. Atherton, Esq., five years ; making a sum total of six persons that have filled that office honorably to themselves, and satisfactorily to the town, during the last seventy years.

The postmasters of our town since 1803 have been Wm. Cobb, Esq., Lemuel Scott, Quartus M. Morgan, Benjamin G. Putnam, and Abner Albee (our present incumbent), making only five persons that have held that necessary appointment, for a term of almost seventy years, showing that location and capability have governed the people in nominating their candidates, in preference to party politics.

We have now to add to the fourteen physicians that resided here prior to 1854 the names of George Field, who lived and practised in this town two years ; G. C. Hill, who resided with us ten years, then removed to Keene, N. H. ; C. J. Barbour, who was with us from one to two years ; and Samuel P. French, who came here in 1869, and is with us at the present time, and is the only practising physician residing in town : making, with those that have been mentioned, eighteen different persons that have lived with us, and practised their profession, since the town was first settled.

Dr. Amos Taylor, who has been mentioned twice in this volume, deserves something more than a passing notice from us; for he lived with us a half-century, and practised his profession in a discreet and acceptable manner for over forty years. He died April 28, 1865, aged eighty years. While he was with us, he was a careful and esteemed physician, an honored citizen, a true friend, a sincere Christian, and an honest man. And before closing this account of the late physicians of Warwick, we will quote an extract from the Rev. P. Smith's semi-centennial sermon where he speaks of Dr. Medad Pomeroy, who was a contemporary with the Rev. Mr. Hedge, a near neighbor and an intimate friend. "Dr. Pomeroy was a native of Northampton, and a graduate of Yale College in 1759. He died October, 1819, five years after my settlement, at the advanced age of eighty-three years. He gave me many interesting reminiscences of his beloved pastor, and of those early times, truly 'days of small things,' when both united their efforts to advance the best interests of the new town, both religious and material. Often, when he was attending patients whose means of comfort were small, Mr. Hedge would fill his saddle-bags with such things as were timely and necessary. Dr. Pomeroy's sympathies were very tender for the afflicted; and on funeral occasions he was expected to have a seat with the mourners, not unfrequently mingling with his tears words of Christian consolation. His kind feelings to all endeared to him a large circle of friends. He was also distinguished for a generous hospitality. Dr. Pomeroy used to repeat to his friends the following lines, as an expression of his hospitable heart:—

> "'To my best my friends are free,
> Free with that, and free with me;
> Free to pass the timely joke,
> And *the tube* sedately smoke;

>   Free to act, and free to think,
>   (No informers with me drink);
>   Free to stay a night or so,
>   And, when uneasy, free to go.' "

HYMN OF WELCOME.

BY MISS M. A. REED.

Friend and Pastor, thou who ever
  Helped to tune our lips to praise,
We, with willing hearts and voices,
  Greet thee with glad welcome lays.
Here thy church, our place of worship;
  Here the people of thy care:
Welcome! welcome! faithful pastor;
  Lead again our praise and prayer.

Fifty years, with all their changes
  Deep inwrought on time's bright scroll,
Here to-day, on memory's tablet,
  Gently backward seem to roll.
Once again we seem to see thee,
  As by Christ-like faith sustained,
In thy manhood's strength and vigor,
  To thy life's great work ordained.

Girded with the Christian's armor,
  Thy great mission just begun,
Through long years of patient labor,
  Still we see thee pressing on.
Guiding erring feet from danger,
  Telling weary ones of rest,
Leading onward, pointing upward,
  To the haven of the blest.

Fifty years! where are the faces
  That were wont to greet us? where?
Where the voices wont to mingle
  In our praise, and in our prayer?
They like autumn leaves are scattered:
  Some afar on life's broad sea,
Some in foremost ranks of battle,
  Some at home, O God! with thee.

Fifty years, dear Christian pastor,
  One by one swift circling round,
Have thy life with bright-hued glories
  Of life's autumn richly crowned.
Soon thy weary steps will linger
  Close beside our Father's door:
Then thou'lt hear a glorious welcome
  On that happy heavenly shore.

WARWICK, Oct. 12, 1864.

RECORD OF MARRIAGES AND INTENTIONS OF MARRIAGE.

FOUND IN THE DIARY OF JONA. BLAKE, JUN., OF WARWICK.

Dec. 7, 1806. Joel Mayo and Abigail Reed, married in Meeting-house by Rev. Samuel Reed.
May 13, 1807. Dr. Ebenezer Hall, married.
" 20, " C. Rich, married.
" 31, " Samuel Williams, married.
June 4, " Clark Stearns and Hannah Leonard, married.
Dec. 10, " Jonas Leonard and Patty Davis, married.
Feb. 11, 1808. Mary Champney, married.
Mar. 9, 1809. Benjamin Conant, 4th, married.
Mar. 18, 1810. Lois Stevens, married.
Oct. 31, · " Joseph Willson and Eunice Ball, married.
Nov. 22, " Mr. Daniel Cook and Widow Goodell, married.

APPENDIX.

Dec. 11, 1810. Mr. Samuel Mayo, married.
Apr. 14, 1811. Levi Smith and Lydia Cobb, married.
Aug. 21, " Cummins Lesure and Polly Ball, married.
Sept. 29, " Isaiah Bridge and Sukey Davis, married.
Oct. 9, " Anna Stevens, married.
Nov. 19, " Mr. Levi Gage and Nancy Barnes, married.
" 21, " William B. Stow and Lucy Moore, married in the meeting-house.
" 26, " Jos. Williams, Jr., and Patty Williams, married.
Jan. 21, 1812. Asa Melendy and Sally Moore, married.
Oct. 12, " Betsy Champney, married.
Nov. 17, " Zebiah Williams, married.
Jan. 2, 1814. Joseph Willson and Nancy Reed, married.
Mar. 31, " Stephen Johnson and Polly White, married.
Apr. 10, " Artemas Baker and Elizabeth Bird, married by Jonathan Blake, Jr.
" 14, " Aaron Leland and Lucy Smith, married by Jonathan Blake, Jr.
Nov. 10, " David Rich and Lucretia Mayo, married.
Feb. 1, 1815. Elijah Wrisley and Polly Bancroft, married by Jonathan Blake, Jr.
Mar. 6, " Caleb Hastings and Huldah Penniman, married.
" 8, " Susannah Gould, married.
May 30, " Willard Packard and Hannah Smith, married by Jonathan Blake, Jr.
Apr. 17, 1817. John Bowman, married.
Sept. 29, " Jonathan Shepardson and Hannah Delvee, married.
" 29, " Artemas Brown and Patience Bancroft, married.
Dec. 4, " Lemuel Wheelock and Rhoda Chamberlain, married.
July 8, 1818. Moses M. Reed and Hannah M. Hazeltine, married.
" 13, " Stephen Cobb and Laura Howard, married.
Aug. 26, " Joseph Goddard of Orange entered his intentions with Maria Moore.
" 27, " George Oliver, Esq., and Deborah White, married.

Nov. 25, 1818. Elkanah Whipple, his intentions with Elizabeth Stearns.
Dec. 3, " John Ball, Jr., his intentions with Harriet Moore, and was married in the meeting-house Jan. 3, 1819.
" 6, " Nathan Stevens of Barre, his intentions with Lois Stevens.
" 16, " Samuel Howe of Framingham, and Sally Hastings, married by Jonathan Blake, Jr.
Feb. 2, 1819. Benjamin Perry, his intentions with Hannah Dean.
" 15, " George Jeseph and Mary West, married by Jonathan Blake, Jr.
Mar. 17, " David Barry, his intentions with Sarah Munroe.
Apr. 7, " David Battles, his intentions with Eunice Pickering.
" 18, " Harvey Woods and Sally Pierce, married by Jonathan Blake, Jr.
July 16, " Dean Lincoln, his intentions with Mrs. Elizabeth Eager.
Oct. 10, " Warren Atwood, his intentions with Eliza Stockwell.
" 23, " Stephen Reed, his intentions with Jerusha Moore.
" 30, " Samuel T. Delvee, his intentions with Betsy Ball.
Nov. 3, " John Whitney, Jr., his intentions with Abigail Foster.
Feb. 10, 1820. Levi Stimpson, his intentions with Eliza Proctor.
Mar. 1, " William Hastings, his intentions with Mary Dutton of Windham, Vt.
" 2, " Eliphalet Kingman, his intentions with Mehetable Allen.
" 4, " Hori Waistcoat, his intentions with Clarissa Fisher of Royalston.
Apr. 7, " Stephen J. Kendal, his intentions with Ruth B. Fisher of Royalston.
" 15, " George Fisher, his intentions with Ruth Woodward of Petersham.

APPENDIX.

May 1, 1820. Henry Whipple, his intentions with Polly Smith.
Sept. 9, " Jonas Hill, his intentions with Lucretia Moore.
" 21, " Daniel Smith, his intentions with Melinda Taft of Richmond, N.H.
Oct. 1, " Samuel Blake and Betsy Fay, married by Rev. Preserved Smith.
Jan. 13, 1821. David Ball entered his intentions of marriage with Elizabeth Rice.
" 23, " Amory Mayo entered his intentions of marriage with Sophronia Cobb.
Feb. 4, " Isaac Metcalf of Royalston entered his intentions of marriage with Mrs. Anna M. Rich.
" 10, " Reuben Harrington of Orange, his intentions of marriage with Abigail Abbot.
Aug. 1, " Jonathan Blake, Jr., and Mrs. Betsy Ballard, married at Greenfield.
Sept. 3, " Ezekiel Ellis, his 'intentions with Tamazine Whitmore.
Nov. 17, " Dean Penniman, his intentions with Hannah Hastings.
Jan. 19, 1822. Chapin Holden, his intentions with Lucy Jackson; and they were married Feb. 5, 1822, by Jonathan Blake, Jr.
Apr. 4, " Abraham P. Sherman, intentions with Polly Fay.
May 18, " Thomas Chase, Jr., intentions with Rebecca Chase.
June 25, " Joshua T. Sanger, intentions with Martha H. Leonard.
July 25, " Joseph Williams, Jr., intentions with Hannah J. Mann.
Sept. 7, " Moseley Clapp, intentions with Emelia Burnett.
Nov. 30, " James Ball, Jr., intentions with Clarissa Ball.
Feb. 5, 1823. Jonathan Jackson, intentions with Mrs. Lucy Wheeler.
" 27, " Cushing Lincoln and Mrs. Mara Gale, married by Jonathan Blake, Jr.
Mar. 9, " William Proctor, intentions with Anna Fay.
" 29, " Daniel Johnson, intentions with Almira Porter.

Apr. 16, 1823. Seth Stratton, intentions with Freedom A. Holton.
" 21, " Adams Batchelder, intentions with Clarissa Hastings.
May 10, " Daniel Pratt, intentions with Bathsheba Delvee.
Sept 18, " Rev. P. Smith, intentions with Tryphena W. Goldsbury.
Oct. 1, " Amory Pierce, intentions with Sophronia Barnes.
" 3, " Samuel Abbot, intentions with Abigail Jones of Templeton.
" 12, " Anson Lyman, intentions with Katharine R. Murdock.
" 31, " George Bacheller, intentions with Nancy Pomeroy Pond.
Jan. 16, 1824. Willard Barnes, intentions with Delight Rice of New Salem.
Feb. 28, " Humphrey Wheelock, intentions with Sophia Lesure.
Mar. 6, " Sylvanus Ward, intentions with Anna Draper.
" 21, " John Holman of Royalston, intentions with Eliza Estey.
Apr. 11, " Elias Knolton, intentions with Mrs. Polly Cook.
May 29, " Elisha Rich, intentions with Caroline G. Parker of Winchester, N.H.
June 4, " Samuel Hammond entered his intentions with Mary R. Thayer.
" 21; " Joel Leonard and Abigail Delvee, married.
Sept. 13, ". Silas Lewis, intentions with Sabrina Conant; and they were married Jan. 9, 1825, by Jonathan Blake, Jr.
Oct. 3, " Ebenezer Bird, Jr., intentions with Sarah Knolton.
" 3, " Alexander Blake, intentions with Polly Ward and they were married Nov. 18, 1824, by Jonathan Blake, Jr.
" 5, " Henry Willard and Mrs. Sally Wood, married by Jonathan Blake, Jr.
Dec. 6, " Joseph W. Chase of Royalston, intentions with Melinda Gale.

APPENDIX.

Dec. 31, 1824. Jonas Conant, intentions with Anna Barker of Brattleboro', Vt.
Jan. 21, 1825. Asa Robbins, Jr., and Loving Collar, both of Northfield, married by Jonathan Blake, Jr.
Feb. 3, " James Pierce and Cyntha Bacheller of Warwick, married by Jonathan Blake, Jr.
" 24, " Eliphaz Gould, intentions with Betsey Simonds.
Mar. 4, " Daniel Woodbury of Royalston, intentions with Persis Chase.
" 7, " Jonathan Shepardson of Royalston, intentions with Nancy Jeseph.
" 12, " Capt. Josiah Proctor, intentions with Polly Thompson of Royalston.
Apr. 20, " Reuel Collar and Hannah Chapin, both of Northfield, married by Jonathan Blake, Jr.
Sept. 2, " Amory Gale, Jr., intentions with Patty Leland.
" 29, " Lorenzo Lord of Orange, intentions with Olive Moore.
" 29, " Gardner Conant, intentions with Livonia Hodge.
Oct. 18, " Mr. Joseph Goodell (aged 90 years) and Mrs. Sarah Woodcock of Royalston, married.
" 23, " David Clark, intentions with Hannah Fisher.
" 29, " David Burnet, intentions with Marcia Grout of Richmond, N.H.
Nov. 20, " John Smith and Lois Jeseph, married by Jonathan Blake, Jr.
" 27, " Elder John Shepardson, intentions with Abigail Lawrence of New Salem.
Dec. 2, " Jonathan Gardner, intentions with Abigail Cole.
" 9, " William Frye of Bolton, intentions with Fanny Fuller.
" 11, " Andrew Russell, intentions with Melinda Fay.
Jan. 13, 1826. Edward Mayo entered his intention of marriage with Eunice Ball.
" 21, " Aaron Bass entered his intention of marriage with Mrs. Betsey Rice.
Feb. 2, " Isaac Hastings, Jr., entered his intention of marriage with Prudence Hallory of Winchester, N.H.

Mar. 20, 1826. Wheaton Kelton of Winchester, N.H., with Mary Ann Bishop of Warwick.
July 20, " Jacob Collar of Northfield, with Betsey Smith of Warwick.
Aug. 23, " Elisha Brown, Jr., with Almira Cole.
" 29, " Henry Sawyer of Lancaster, with Catharine B. Burnett of Warwick.
Sept. 2, " Ichabod D. Battle of Orange, with Miranda Moore of Warwick.
" 9, " Joseph. Williams, with Mrs. Lucy Pratt.
Oct. 13, " Dennis Fay, with Adaline H. Flagg of Holden.
Nov. 19, " Samuel T. Delvee, with Rebecca Stockwell.
Dec. 2, " James Goldsbury, with Miranda Sweetser of Athol.
" 9. " Charles Barber of Northfield, with Mary E. Williams of Warwick.
Mar. 24. 1827. John C. Washburn, with Aroe Clark, both of Warwick; and they were married April 19, by Jonathan Blake, Jr.
May 5, " Seth Woodard, Jr., with Lucy or Arethusa Holman of Orange; and they were married June 10, by Jonathan Blake, Jr.
July 16, " Melzar Williams, with Scybinda Wheelock.
Sept. 14, " Samuel Gilson of Erving's Grant, with Achsah Burnett of Warwick.
Oct. 4, " Amory Bartlett of Chesterfield, N.H., with Meriam Conant.
" 28, " Jasper Leland, with Harriet Ann Bass.
Dec. 8, " Rev. Nahum Gould of Macdonnough, N.Y.; with Rebecca B. Leonard; married Jan. 29, 1828.
" 14, " John Adams Green, with Lucy Delvee; and were married Jan. 1, 1828, by Jonathan Blake, Jr.
Jan. 17, 1828. John Goodell Watts, with Mary Foster.
" 17, " Elijah Fisk, with Experience Wheelock.
Apr. 12, " Clement Smith Johnson of New Salem, with Hannah Hazeltine Gale of Warwick.
May 3, " Alpheus Eastman of Hollis, N.H., with Sally Williams of Warwick.

July 1, 1828. David Rich, with Mrs. Elizabeth Chesebrough; and was married Aug. 3, by Jonathan Blake, Jr.
Aug. 4, " William E. Russell, with Mary Ann Pomroy.
" 23, " David Burnett entered his intentions with Lydia Fulton of New Salem.
Sept. 5, " Asa Taft, with Nancy Burnap of Nelson, N.H.
Oct. 26, " Joseph Ball, with Jerusha Hale, both of Warwick.
Apr. 18, 1830. Daniel Evans and Mehetable Cook, married by Jonathan Blake, Jr.
Dec. 12, 1831. Benjamin Merriam and Mrs. Polly Carter, married by Jonathan Blake, Jr.
Jan. 11, 1832. Alexander Burnett and Eliza Burnett, married by Jonathan Blake, Jr.
May 23, " George W. Moore and Sarah P. Leonard, married by Jonathan Blake, Jr.
" 27, " Ichabod Whipple and Fanny Simonds, married by Jonathan Blake, Jr.
" 29, " Noah Adams of Winchester, N.H., and Eunice Stearns, married by Jonathan Blake, Jr.
Nov. 1, " Hervey Barber and Hannah Leland, married.
Jan. 8, 1833. Alvah C. Page and Mary Ann Blake, married.
June 2, " Artemas Murdock, Jr., and Mary Simonds, married by Jonathan Blake, Jr.
Sept. 20, 1835. Samuel Nute and Sarah Ann Delvee, married by Jonathan Blake, Jr.
Nov. 3, " Asa H. Conant and Semira Fuller, married.
Dec. 21, 1836. Benjamin F. Dean and Mary Ann Russell, married.
" 22, " Keith White and Mary H. Goodell, married.
Nov. 28, 1839. James H. Clapp and Leonora Blake, married by Rev. Preserved Smith.
" 28, " Artemas B. Fuller and Ophelia Packard, married by Rev. Roger C. Hatch.
Dec. 2, " Samuel Fay, Jr., and Sarah Taylor.
May 17, 1840. Frederic Clapp and Martha M. Blake, married by Rev. Preserved Smith.
Nov. 29, " Ibri Baker and Eliza Barber, married.
Jan. 5, 1841. Mr. —— Furbush and Sarah Fisher, married.

Jan.   6, 1841. Mark Foster and Sarah Nash, married.
Apr. 20,   "   Stillman Barber and Mary Fisher, married.
May 31,   "   Dea. Hervey Barber and Ann M. Child, married.
Oct.   3. "   Joseph W. Green and Mary Ann Ball, married.
Nov. 15,   "   James E. Blake and Relief Smith, married by Rev. Preserved Smith.
Nov. 7, 1842. Alfred Nutter and Charlotte Mayo, married.
Feb. 1, 1843. Lewis A. Drury and Sarah C. Gilbert, married by Jonathan Blake.
July 4, 1844. Benjamin F. Fuller and Mary Green, married.

RECORD OF DEATHS IN WARWICK.

COPIED FROM JONA. BLAKE'S DIARY.

1807.
Feb. 13, Frederick Barnes.
 "   23, Mr. Peter Delvee.
May 11, Mary Ann Blake.
June 12, Martin Maynard.
July 8, Mr. J. Weeks, accident.
Aug. 10, Mrs. Davis.
Oct. 6, Dr. Ellis.
Nov. 8, Harriet Mayo.
 "   28, David Bancroft.
1808.
Jan. 6, Lucy Haven.
 "   13, John Goodell.
 "   19, Josiah Rawson.
 "   24, E. Rawson's child.
 "   30, Capt. Jonathan Gale.
April 2, Old Mrs. Mallard.
June 22, Samuel Lesure's daughter.
Sept. 4, Mrs. Ager's child.
Oct. 21, Thomas Tuel.
Nov. 26, John W. Mayo.
Dec. 1, Mrs. Daniel Cook.

Dec. 12, Mrs. Samuel Mayo.
1809.
Feb. 1, Semira Cobb.
 "   20, Lydia Streeter.
Mar. 10, Mr. Isaiah Fuller.
 "   13, Perez Allen's child.
May 2, Jno. Moore, Jr.'s, wife.
Sept. 14, Ebenezer Pierce's wife.
Nov. 2, Mr. Thomas Gould.
1810.
Mar. 6, Jno. Moore, Jr.'s, son.
 "   12, Joseph Severy.
Apl. 17, Rich. Waistcoat's child.
 "   25, Seneca Whitney.
May 2, Mr. —— Thornton.
 "   6, Mr. Abijah Fisher.
 "   21, Mr. Jacob White.
Oct. 2, Lewis Atwood.
Nov. 20, James Ball's son.
 "   27, Captain Elisha Hunt of Northfield.
Dec. 6, Mr. Griffith, State paup.
 "   30, Joel Jennings's child.

APPENDIX. 215

1811.
Feb. 4, Mr. Daniel Cook.
" 24, Fanny Ball.
" 24, Wm. Burnet, 3d.
Apl. 29, Thomas Bancroft's wife.
June 16, Mr. James Stockwell.
" 27, Reuben Gale.
July 14, Mrs. Eaton.
Aug. 17, Richard Waistcoat.
" 29, Mr. William Cobb.
Sept. 21, —— Severence.
" 29, Mrs. Johnson.
Nov. 4, Azariah Barber's wife.
" 28, Jonathan Goddard of Orange, by hanging himself on an apple-tree.
Dec. 14, Nancy Moore, at Brookline.
" 17, Capt. Charles Rich.
1812.
Jan. 7, Fanny Bancroft.
Feb. 5, Mrs. Jonas Clark.
" 6, Old Mr. Weeks.
" 6, Mrs. —— Stone.
Mar. 7, Old Mrs. Bass.
" 12, Mrs. Martha Conant, aged 59 yrs. 8 mos.
" 31, Mr. Enoch Kilton, aged 86 years.
April 9, Mrs. Nathan Kilton.
" 17, Joseph Willson's wife.
May 16, Polly Fay.
June 4, Eph. Robbins, Jr.'s, wife.
" 6, Med. Pomeroy, Jr.'s, son.
" 13, Eunice Leonard.
" 22, Polly Bowman.
July 31, Rev. Samuel Reed.
Nov. 3, Patience Barber.
" 20, Jos. Williams, Jr.'s, wife.
1813.
Jan. 4, Mr. Hen. Field of Northfield.

Jan. 17, Betsey Whitney.
Mar. 6, Samuel Moore's child.
" 31, Levi Maynard's wife.
May 4, Sibil Leonard.
June 3, Mrs. H. G. Stevens.
July 19, David Ball's son.
" 30, Francis Leonard's second daughter.
Aug. 26, Ebenr. Bancroft's wife.
1814.
Feb. 16, Mr. Samuel Eveleth.
" 17, Mrs. Rawson.
" 19, Abner Goodell's son.
Mar. 11, Joshua Atwood's wife.
June 5, Wm. Lewis's dau.
" 8, Mr. Ebenezer Bancroft.
" 24, Old Mrs. Proctor.
Oct. 23, Mr. Minard, glassblower.
Nov. 4, L. N. Wood's son.
" 27, Daniel Peck of Royalston, 74 yrs.
Dec. 15, Olive Cook.
" 29, Elona Daniels.
1815.
Jan. 11, Dea. Benjamin Conant.
Feb. 3, Eunice Leonard, 6 mos.
" 4, Old Mrs. Stearns.
" 12, Mr. Jesse Warrick.
Apl. 16, Mrs. Taylor, wife of Walter.
1816.
Nov. 13, Francis Leonard, 6 mos.
" 17, Job Maycumber.
" 27, Old Mrs. Jennings.
Dec. 20, Melinda Daniels, 24 yrs.
1817.
Jan. 10, Mrs. Cobb.
Feb. 7, Phillip Atwood's wife.
" 15, Ephraim Tuel.
Mar. 5, Mr. Jacob Rich.
" 22, Josiah Proctor's infant child.

Mar. 23, Daniel Collar's child.
" 25, Mr. Robert Eaton, 83 yrs.
April 3, Joseph Barber's wife.
June 18, Mr. Jesse Gale.
" 18, Mr. Jno. Shepardson.
Aug. 19, Rev. P. Smith's daughter, born and died.
Sept. 13, Mercy Conant.
" 18, Dr. Lemuel Barnard, 81 yrs.
Dec. 8, Henry Burnet.

1818.
Jan. 12, Benj. Hastings, suicide.
Feb. 3, Moses Leonard, 81 yrs. 6 days.
" 17, Mrs. Litchfield.
May 5, Samuel Barnes's wife.
Sept. 25, Lucy Leonard, 27 yrs.
Dec. 17, Ezekiel Cook, 39 yrs.
" 21, Mrs. Hurd.

1819.
Jan. 13, Joseph Steven's wife, 22 years.
Apr. 12, David Ball's wife.
" 18, Nancy Bangs.
May 31, Melinda Knolton.
June 12, Old Mr. Fay, 79 years.
July 31, Amos Fisher, drowned.
Aug. 4, Stephen Cobb.
" 28, Olive Howard.
Sept. 7, Mr. Moses Fisher.
Oct. 21, Mrs. Patty Blake, 33 yrs.
" 28, Dr. Medad Pomeroy, 83 years.
Nov. 27, Benj. Simond's wife.
Dec. 21, Mr. Samuel Bowman, 70 years.

1820.
Jan. 3, Roxana Allen.
" 17, Mr. N. Cook, 71 years.
" 19, Mrs. Jackson.
Feb. 14, Harriet Draper.

Feb. 19, Old Mr. Bachelder.
Mar. 21, Benj. Lincoln Bangs.
" 30, Mr. Jacob Packard.
Apr. 6, Widow Clarissa Gale.
Sept. 1, Mrs. Elona Conant.
Oct. 6, Asa Thayer's wife.
" 23, Elijah Fisk's wife.

1821.
Jan. 24, J. Williams, Jr.'s, wife.
May 1, Mary Whitney.
" 3, Mr. Daniel Whitney.
June 5, Capt. Asa Thayer.
Aug. 17, Mr. Josiah Pomeroy, 80 years.
Sept. 5, Old Mrs. Goldsbury.

1822.
Jan. 1, Mr. Zacheriah Barber.
" 5, Widow Lydia Fisher, 38 years.
" 5, Mr. David Perry.
Mar. 2, Daniel M. Johnson.
June 16, Mrs. Bebe Smith.
Dec. 17, Wid. Anna Leonard, 77 years.

1823.
Jan. 1, Old Mrs. Wheelock.
Mar. 17, Wm. Tripp, killed by a tree.
" 21, Sarah Cobb.
Apr. 6, Mrs. Hannah Bishop.
June 20, Mrs. Mason.
" 28, Mr. Joshua Atwood.
July 20, Mrs. Sally Proctor.
" 23, Mrs. Sally Conant.
Aug. 4, Mr. Ebenezer Stearns.
" 13, Old Mrs. Perry.
Sept. 2, Maria Mayo.
Dec. 18, Joseph Metcalf, Esq.

1824.
Mar. 2, Mrs. Bowman.
May 29, Old Mrs. Delvee.
July 31, Harriet Leonard.

APPENDIX.   217

Sept. 6, Mr. Richard Cobb.
" 20, Widow Sarah Whitney.
Oct. 31, Mr. Daniel Wiswell.
Nov. 6, Lois Whitney.
" 12, James B. Leonard.
1825.
Feb. 14, Mrs. Sibil Smith.
" 19, Mr. Wm. Simonds, 63 years.
" 19, Gen. Arad Hunt of Vernon.
" 20, Old Mrs. Goodell.
Mar. 2, Mr. Lemuel Hastings of Greenfield.
May 23, Mr. Samuel Mayo.
June 5, Mr. Daniel Bancroft.
" 5, Mrs. Esther Russell.
July 19, Mrs. Gardner.
" 21, John Bunyan Penniman.
Sept. 12, Capt. John Pratt.
Dec. 21, Mrs. Polly, wife of Sam'l Williams.
" 27, Mr. Samuel Lesure.
1826.
Jan. 12, Mr. Abel Eddy.
Feb. 3, Samuel Reed, at Greenfield.
Mar. 19, Mrs. Betsy Delvee.
Apr. 15, Jas. Ball's wife, suicide.
May 15, Samuel Barnes, at New Salem.
Aug. 2, Wilder Stevens, 79 yrs.
" 21, Capt. Lesure's wife.
" 25, Joel Mayo's wife, 41 yrs.
Sept. 9, Henry Leland, 76 yrs.
" 29, John Batcheller, 80 yrs.
Oct. 12, Dr. Benjamin Hazeltine.
1827.
Mar. 13, David Burnett's wife.
May 13, Betsey Blake, wife of Samuel.

May 15, Sally Hastings.
" 21, Betsey H. Ball, dau. of Stephen.
July 8, Lyman Knolton.
Aug. 6, Lieut. Ebenr. Stearn's child.
Oct. 15, Fanny Cook.
Dec. 6, James Stockwell.
1828.
Jan. 5, Mr. Jonathan Moore.
" 5, Mrs. David Rich.
Feb. 12, Deacon Eben'r Pierce.
" 23, Mrs. Lucy Fay.
Oct. 30, Widow Jones.
Nov. 5, John Whitney, Jr.'s, child.
Dec. 17, Old Mrs. Bangs.
1829.
Mar. 17, Jos. Goodell, about 94 yrs.
" 20, Harriet, dau. of A. K. Whitney.
" 21, Mrs. Burnett, wife of Andrew.
May 10, Mary Fuller.
July 6, Asa Atwood's wife.
Dec. 10, Mason, son of Joseph Leonard, Jr.
1830.
Jan. 4, Joel Pierce, two infant children.
" 5, Mrs. Tryphena Dutton.
" 18, Mrs. Lydia Pierce.
May 20, Levi Stearns (town pau.)
July 3, Mrs. Allen, wife of Calvin Allen.
Oct. 16, Henry Fuller.
Nov. 13, Mrs. Francis Leonard.
Dec. 17, Hannah Whitney, 26 yrs.
1831.
Feb. 21, George Mason.
Mar. 8, Capt. Eleazer Wheelock, 81 yrs.

19

Mar 29, Mr. Reuben Wheaton.
Apr. 28, Jane Kendrick (pauper).
May 11, Hannah Fuller.
July 25, Eunice Morse.
Aug. 1, William, son of Charles C. Cobb.
" 5, Serepta Wyman.
" 6, David Rich's child, 1 yr.
" 10, Abel Sanger, 38 yrs.
" 13, John Whitney, Jr.'s, youngest child.
" 15, Mrs. Sarah Blake, 80 yrs. 8 mos.
" 19, John Whitney, Jr.'s, dau.
" 19, Nancy Bowman, 42 yrs.
" 19, John Bowman's child.
" 21, Mehetable Kelton, wife of Thomas, 84 yrs. 7 mos.
" 23, Hannah Holden.
" 30, Mr. John Bowman.
" 30, A child of Mr. John Bowman.
Sept. 2, Wid. Mary Fuller, 80 yrs.
" 8, Rebecca Perry, 3 yrs.
" 14, Clark Ware, 24 yrs.
" 25, Mr. Isaac Hastings.
" 27, Mrs. Whitney, wife of John, Jr.
Oct. 9, Mrs. Rebecca Packard (pauper).
" 25, Charles E., son of Alexander Blake, 23 mos.
1832.
Feb. 11, Elisha M. Davis's child.
" 21, Mr. Asa Conant, 82 yrs.
Mar. 5, Ebenr. Barber's child.
" 5, Justus Russell, Jr., 31 yrs.
" 18, Mr. Samuel Abbott, 39 yrs.
" 23, Mr. Shelding's child.

Mar. 27, Capt. Mark Moore, 83 yrs.
Apr. 13, Mr. Nathl. G. Stevens, 80 yrs.
" 30, John C. Miller (pauper).
May 14, Mr. Amaziah Kelton.
June 6, Ebenr. Barber's wife.
" 21, Old Mrs. Burnett.
July 29, Josiah Proctor, Jr.
Aug. 31, Col. Abner Goodell, 50 yrs.
Sept. 6, David Burnett's child.
Oct. 30, Old Mrs. Pomroy, 86 yrs.
1833.
Mar. 7, Mr. Thomas Hurd, 74 yrs.
Apr. 4, Abijah Fisher, 76 yrs.
July 5, Mrs. Fanny Whipple.
" 18, Mr. Nathan Leonard, 70 yrs.
" 22, Old Mrs. Thankful White (pauper).
Aug. 14, Old Mrs. Robbins, 89 yrs.
Nov. 4, Old Mrs. Richards.
" 20, Mrs. Mary Ann Page, 23 yrs.
Dec. 11, John Pierce of Dorchester, 91 yrs.
1834.
Jan. 25, Old Mr. Samuel Moses's wife.
May 30, Jona. Delvee, Jr.'s, child.
June 11, Elvira Leonard.
Aug. 7, Joseph G. Whitney.
" 15, Rev. Preserved Smith, 75 yrs.
" 21, Mary Atwood.
1835.
Jan. 7, Isaac Pierce, 71 yrs.
Mar. 3, Mrs. Jerusha Ball, wife of Joseph Ball.

APPENDIX. 219

Mar. 9, Mrs. Griffith (pauper).
" 24, Mr. William Burnett, 93 yrs.
Apr. 29, Mr. Henry Fuller, 55 yrs.
July 18, Mrs. Tryphena Smith, 34 yrs.
Aug. 29, Wid. Lois Fisher.
Dec. 1, Mrs. Betsey Bass, by suicide.
" 6, Mrs. Nancy Willson.
1836.
Mar. 4, John Ball, Jr., by suicide.
" 23, Mr. Abijah Eddy, 60 yrs.
Oct. 8, Mr. Jonathan Blake, 87 yrs. 9 mos. 8 days.
Dec. 24. Mary Ann Fisher (pau.)
1837.
Jan. 1, Harris Fuller, 27 yrs.
" 27, Patty Brown.
Mar. 19, Wid. Rebecca Moore, 88 yrs.
May 19, Mr. Jonas Leonard, 91 yrs.
June 3, Henry H. Conant, 9 mos
Oct. 20, Dea. Ebenezer Stearns, 60 yrs.
1838.
Apr. 8, Mrs. Betsey Ball, 56 yrs.
May 20, Daniel Green's youngest child.
" 27, Samuel G. Robbins's child.
July 5, Mr. Stephen Ball, 63 yrs
" 7, Daniel Green's child.
Aug. 17, Asa H. Conant's child.
Sept 4, Sally Mayo, 54 yrs.
Oct. 13, David Gale, Jr.'s, son Amos.
" 20, David Gale, Jr.'s, youngest child.
1839.
Jan. 2, Emily P. White.

Jan. 10, David Godard's wife.
" 25, Rhoda Cook
Feb. 13, Wid. Polly Drake, 47 yrs.
Sept. 8, Wid. —— Rich.
" 26, Nancy Blake, 51 yrs, 6 mos. 20 days.
Oct. 18, Capt. Joseph Ball, 50 yrs., fell from the bridge at Miller's River when raising it.
1840.
Feb. 1, Samuel Cobb, 57 yrs.
Mar. 23, Wid. Nathaniel Stearns, 86 yrs.
Aug. 24, Mrs. H. Barber, wife of Dea. Hervey, 27½ yrs.
Oct. 4, Martha Proctor, at New Salem.
Dec. 4, Elizabeth Wellman, 38 yrs.
" 8, Samuel Manning's dau. Elizabeth, 3 yrs.
1841.
Jan. 15, Melissa Harvey, 12 yrs.
" 28, Wid. —— Ager, 70 yrs.
Feb. 22, Joseph Williams, 78 yrs.
" 27, Capt. Daniel H. Smith, 65 yrs.
Mar. 14, James H. Horton's child, about 8 mos.
" 17, Dea. Samuel Ball, 72 yrs.
Apr. 13, Mrs. John Ball.
June 20, Mrs. Icibinda Williams, 40 yrs. 8 mos.
July 20, Mr. David Gale, 73 yrs.
Aug. 6, Capt. Cummings Lesure. 55 yrs.
Sept. 1, —— Severence, 18 yrs.
Oct. 8, Mr. Jonas Houghton, 50 yrs.
" 9, Mrs. Mary Baker, wife of Isaac, 27 yrs.

Oct. 9, Miss Anna Whipple, dau. of Henry, 19 years.

1842.
Feb. 12, Mrs. Sarah Severy, a town pauper, very aged.
" 26, Col. Lemuel Wheelock, 51 yrs.
May 4, Mrs. Hannah Smith, wife of Jehiel.
June 21, Israel Fisher, 83 yrs.
Aug. 29, Samuel T. Delvee's youngest child.
" 30, Mr. Morgan's child.
Sept. 16, Gardner P. Mills's child.
" 24, Gardner P. Mills's child.
Dec. 21, Mrs. Grout (wife of Harry).

1843.
Jan. 6, Dea. Francis Leonard, 65 yrs.
" 25, Mr. Elias Knowlton.
Feb. 4, Artemas B. Fuller's wife, 23 yrs.
" 8, Franklin Gould, 4 yrs.
" 22, Henry Hatch, 16 yrs.
Mar. 6, Elisha Severy, a town pauper.
" 6, Fidelia Smith.
" 6, Alfred Moore.
" 20, Timothy Stevens's youngest child.
June 2, Mr. Henry Hastings.
" 25, Mr. William Hastings.
" 28, Mr. Daniel Johnson, by suicide.
Aug. 2, Mr. Philip Atwood, 84 yrs. 7 mos. 2 days.
Nov. 24, Miss Lucy Wheelock, 57 yrs.

1844.
Jan. 6, Foster Bowman, 18 yrs.

Jan. 17, Mr. Thomas Mallard, Jr., 47 yrs.
Feb. 3, Charles Hutchens, at Hawley, 15 yrs.
" 19, Mrs. Smith.
Mar. 24, Christopher Columbus Wheaton Merrifield.
" 30, George King.
Apr. 5, Wid. Sarah Moore.
" 5, Infant child of —— Houghton.
" 20, Calvin W. Delvee's dau.
May 12, Mr. Abram Felton.
June 1, Timothy F. Phillips, 37 yrs.
" 9, Hannah D. Leonard.
Aug. 24, Mrs. Nancy Fay, 63 yrs.
Sept. 30, Wid. Anna Reed, 88 yrs.
Oct. 16, Joseph Delvee's wife.
" 17, Joseph Delvee's infant child.
" 21, Lorenzo Bancroft, 29 yrs.
Dec. 6, Mr. Jonas Leonard, 60 yrs.

1845.
Feb. 8, Azariah Barber, 65 yrs.
" 16, David Howland Goodell, 2 yrs. 5 mos. 12 days.
Mar. 29, Mrs. Fisher (wid. of Israel), 78 yrs.
May 12, Wid. Beulah Cook.
" 23, Wid. Mary Kilburn.
July 13, Elihu Gould.
Sept. 9, Mrs. Susannah Cobb, 95 yrs. 6 mos.
" 28, George Chesebro's infant child.
" 29, Mr. John Green.

1846.
Jan. 17, Austin Mallard, 25 yrs.
" 18, Harriet Thayer.
May 6, —— Gilbert.

APPENDIX. 221

May 7, John Brown's wife, by suicide.
June 28, Sam. Blake's wife, at Lowell, 43 yrs. 5 mos. 6 days.
Sept. 8, Calvin W. Delvee's child, 2 yrs.
" 9, Philander Pierce's child, 16 mos.

Sept. 17, Thomas Blake, 66 yrs. 4 mos.
Oct. 4, Frederic B. Blake, 1 yr. 8 mos.
" 8, Henry D. Green (son of Joseph).
" 22, John B. Blake, 20 yrs. 9 mos. 28 days.

DEATHS IN WARWICK,

FROM JAN. 1, 1847, to 1872.

Taken from the Diary of Dea. Hervey Barber, as a continuation of those taken from that of Hon. J. Blake.

	Yrs.
1847.	
Feb. 5, Mrs. Martha Sanger,	47
Mar. 3, Stephen Reed,	56
Apr. 22, Saml. F. Taylor,	24
June 14, Medad Pomeroy,	70
July 4, Ebenr. Rich,	51
" 15, Parley Leland,	75
Aug. 23, Eldad Hodge,	57
" 24, Sarah Stevens,	17
Sept. 3, Wid. Hannah Houghton,	50
Oct. 11, Dea. James Blake,	73
Nov. 15, Timothy H. Barber,	6
Dec. 25, Wid. Betsey Gould,	51
1848.	
Apr. 1, Wid. Jerusha Goldsbury,	74
" 17, David Goddard,	41
" 27, Enoch Robbins,	83
" 28, Mrs. Ann L. Ball,	23
May 16, Wid. Hannah Whitney,	67
June 19, Elijah Fisk,	74
July 30, Miss Abigail Barber,	53
Aug. 2, Joseph Delvee,	45
" 26, Bunyan Penniman,	76
Oct. 1, Thomas Mallard,	87
Nov. 22, Ashbill Ward, Esq.,	72
Dec. 29, Mrs. Ephraim Robbins,	69
1849.	
Feb. 21, Dau. of C. M. Procter,	3
" 23, Wid. Hammond,	77
Mar. 1, Obadiah Bass,	72
" 29, Mrs. Mary Holton,	33
Apr. 24, Mrs Lavina Conant,	44
May 9, Wid. Esther Fuller,	66
" 9, Dau. of Chas. Pomroy, 7 mos.	
" 9, Endracas Wheeler,	48
June 27, Daniel Evans,	45
" 28, Miss Esther Smith,	24
Aug. 26, Son of Tim. Moore, 10 mos.	
Sept. 21, Miss Parmelia Moore,	21
" 22, Mrs. Elizabeth Taylor,	32

Dec. 15, Ephraim Robbins, 73
1850.
June 23, Miss Ann Whitney, 40
July 27, Mrs. Simonds Smith, 34
Aug. 1, Daniel Holman, 68
" 13, Wid. Jerusha Pomroy, 65
Sept. 19, Dau. of F. C. Taylor, 2 mos.
Oct. 27, Wid. Nabby Wheaton, 76
Nov. 6, Joseph Stevens, Esq., 59
Dec. 15, Jonathan Delvee, 80
1851.
Jan. 16, Mrs. Jonathan Wheelock, 71
" 24, Mrs. A. H. Whitney, 70
Apr. 9, Wid. Polly Delvee, 80
" 14, Mrs. L. F. Burrage, 44
May 12, Nahum Grout, 83
" 13, Mrs. Elisha M. Davis, 41
June 22, James Fuller, 58
Aug. 6, Miss Alma Gale, 19
Sept. 2, Mrs. John Morgan, 26
" 22, Son of Benj. Davis, 6
Nov. 1, Laban Simonds, 69
" 28, Son of John Whipple, 14
Dec. 21, Dau. of Ansel Davis, 6 mos.
1852.
Jan. 12, Miss Sarah Leonard, 39
" 13, Mrs. David Gale, jun. 23
" 15, Mrs. Josiah Conant, 88
" 16, Phinehas Child, jun. 48
Feb. 21, Mrs Melzar Williams, 46
Mar. 4, Martha Delvee, 8
" 6, Son of Ansel Davis, 3
May 1, Jonathan Wheelock, 72
June 6, Elkanah Whipple, 75
" 9, Miss Betsey Delvee, 22
" 22, Mrs. Czarina Wheeler, 29
" 26, Henry Barnard, Esq., 83
July 6, James Holton, 70

July 8, Mrs. Lydia Smith, 63
" 26, Mrs. Maria Fisher, 26
" 31, Geo. F. Taylor, 9
Aug. 13, Miss Rhoda Cook, 83
" 22, Mrs Susanna Child, 79
Sept. 13, Miss Lucy Orcutt, 22
" 29, Amory Gale, 76
Nov. 13, James Holmes, 71
" 23, Mrs. Fanny Barber, 33
Dec. 22, Mrs. Nathan Atwood, 58
" 25, Jonathan Moore, 76
1853.
Jan. 25, Son of James Stockwell, 22 mos.
Mar. 26, Samuel Ball, 57
Apr. 3, Mrs. Bulah Eddy, 69
May 15, Mrs. Robert Adamson, 34
" 23, Mason Davis, 9
June 12, William Cobb, Esq. 83
" 17, Miss Maria Williams, 20
" 22, Elisha Brown, 81
Aug. 21, Mrs. Asa H. Conant, 39
Sept. 4, Mrs. Geo. Dudley, 22
Nov. 17, Miss Lydia Jones, 79
1854.
Feb. 27, Mrs. Nathan C. Morse, 71
Mar. 3, Mrs. Clark Stearns, 33
" 10, An infant son of N. E Stevens, 2 days.
" 29, Amos H. Whitney, 79
May 15, Elizabeth Adams, 12
" 29, Ezekiel Nelson, 78
June 26, Mrs. Ivers Creed, 40
July 24, Anna S. Barber, 22 mos.
Aug. 2, Mrs. Ruth Owen, 22
" 5, Mrs. S. C. Reed, 25
" 12, S. Switzer Goldsbury, 20
Oct. 22, Dau. of Mr. Henry, 1
" 30, Eunice Stearns, 84

APPENDIX. 223

Dec. 10, Mrs. Daniel Whittemore,	75
" 12, Son of Franklin Whitney, 8 weeks.	
" 19, Daniel Whittemore,	84
" 23, Asa Atwood,	71
1855.	
Jan. 9, Mrs. David Gale,	84
" 12, Joseph Draper,	81
" 19, Josiah Conant,	91
" 19, Widow of Thos. Mallard, jun.,	56
Mar. 27, Widow of Elkanah Whipple,	73
Apr. 1, Mrs. Asa Bancroft,	68
May 4, Dau. of Philander Pierce, 11 mos.	
June 23, Caleb Weeks,	79
" 25, Caleb Hastings,	66
July 4, Son of Alfred Brown 2 mos.	
Aug. 8, Miss Lucy Eddy,	79
" 31, Ichabod Whipple,	58
Sept. 18, Rufus Knight,	62
" 25, A. Baker Fuller,	40
Dec. 6, Wid. Amory Gale,	80
Oct. 13, Sarah Shepardson,	16
1856.	
Mar. 14, Mrs. S. W. Gillson,	44
" 18, Son of Richard Weeks,	10
Apr. 8, Miss Ann Ward,	27
" 9, Mrs. Alexander Blake,	53
" 28, Dea. Sylvanus Ward,	54
May 5, Wid. Sylvanus Ward,	54
June 1, Son of S. T. Underwood, 1 day.	
July 15, Mrs. John Farnsworth,	26
Aug. 6, Miss Martha Chase,	23
" 30, Mrs. Hervey Partridge,	68
Sept. 12, Wid. Daniel Smith,	76
Sept. 18, Jonas Conant,	81
Oct. 9, Miss Martha Moore,	37
Dec. 7, Justus Russell, Esq.,	85
1857.	
Jan. 12, Mrs. Paul Jillson,	64
" 20, Stephen Johnson,	79
Mar. 25, Albert Lawrence,	21
Apr. 2, Seth Woodward,	55
June 6, Mrs. Barnard Fisher,	35
" 18, Miss Lucy Shepardson,	69
Aug. 9, Miss Luthera Wheelock,	60
Sept. 1, Miss Ellen Bass,	22
" 7, Ephraim Morgan,	93
Oct. 3, Mrs. Henry Barnard,	83
1858.	
Jan. 29, Mrs. Elkanah Whipple,	67
Apr. 2, Mrs. —— Burnham,	54
May 18, Wid. Stephen Johnson,	75
" 31, Mrs. Wm. Lawrence,	46
June 24, Mrs. Elijah Davis,	78
July 14, Wid. Amariah Kelton,	74
Sept. 29, Lemuel Scott,	33
Oct. 1, H. G. Mallard, Esq.,	29
" 12, Edward Hastings,	28
" 21, Wid. Perley Leland,	85
" 22, Benjamin Drake,	44
Nov. 20, Jehiel Smith,	69
Aug. 29, Miss Anna Goss,	74
1859.	
Jan. 17, Laban Simonds,	73
Feb. 18, Mrs. Chas. William Cobb,	21
Mar. 7, Fannie Phillips,	17
" 16, Wid. Seth Woodward,	58
" 20, Mrs. Hosea Horton,	70
May 27, Ansel Davis,	59

June 13, Miss Rhoda Hodge,	59
July 16, Nathan Atwood,	70
Aug. 21, Miss Forbes,	72
" 25, Simeon Stearns,	80
Nov. 30, Mrs. Cushing Lincoln,	84
1860.	
Jan. 16, Isaac Hastings,	74
" 17, Jona. Gardner Gale,	18
May 31, Mrs. Almira Fry,	42
July 20, Mrs. Elizabeth C. Bird,	50
Aug. 31, John Smith,	72
Oct. 29, Paul Jillson,	71
Nov. 3, Henry Harvey,	60
Aug. 28, Henry Gale,	13
1861.	
Jan. 25, Wid. Stephen Reed,	69
" 27, Sarah Shepardson,	16
" 28, Jane Shepardson,	10
Feb. 6, Mrs. Simon P. Shepardson,	41
" 20, Nye Shepardson,	13
Mar. 5, Miss Sophia Whitney,	83
" 30, Samuel T Delvee,	68
July 20, Henry C. Conant,	23
Aug. 1, Mrs. Josiah Conant,	59
" 11, Ira Ager,	53
" 11, Elijah Davis,	87
" 31, Mrs. Q. M. Morgan,	47
Oct. 2, Wid. James Stockwell,	78
" 21, Dau. of Saml. Reed, 3 weeks.	
Nov. 9, Cushing Lincoln,	87
" 24, Wid. John Bowman,	63
Dec. 26, Jasper H. Leland,	27
" 31, John Stearns,	81
1862.	
Jan. 8, Wid. Elisha Brown,	88
Feb. 24, Leander Jillson,	18
Feb. 24, Willard Packard,	24
Mar. 12 and 17, Son and dau. of Wm. Ward.	
" 29, Hervey Partridge,	72
June 20, Wid. of Dea. J. Proctor,	77
May 9, Wid. Nathan Leonard,	88
July 26, Stanley Cushing,	19
Aug. 9, Mrs. Joseph Wilson,	67
Sept. 2, Mrs. Philander Pierce,	43
" 28, Francis Moore,	20
Oct. 8, Wid. Bunyan Penniman,	88
" 23, Miss Maria Conant,	43
Nov. 18, Peter Severance,	47
Dec. 21, Frank Pierce,	21
1863.	
Feb 2, Samuel Moore,	67
Apr. 13, Aaron Bass,	80
" 25, James Chapin,	20
" 26, Wid. Field,	83
" 27, Mrs. George Jones,	69
May 4, Miss Fanny Gould,	69
" 15, Mrs. Lafayette Nelson,	30
" 22, Miss Hannah Burnett,	23
" 23, David Gale,	68
June 28, Jacob S. Rayner, jun.,	18
July 7, Abbie J. Reed,	6
" 8, Warren Blake,	20
Aug. 14, Wid. Jonas Leonard,	76
" 25, John Caldwell,	20
Sept 1, Edmund Coller,	20
Oct. 15, Munro Patridge,	21
" 27, Lafayette Nelson,	36
" 27, Wid. Elias Knowlton,	86
1864.	
Jan. 22, Hattie Phillips,	16
" 29, Geo. W. Howard,	49
Feb. 8, Miss Lydia Ball,	82
Mar. 12, Wid. William Cobb,	91

… APPENDIX. 225

Date	Name	Age
Apr. 6,	Joseph B Atwood,	23
May 10,	Ivers Creed,	41
June 4,	Wid. James Fuller,	72
" 18,	Seth A. Woodward,	30
July 13,	Lucy Ann Brown,	15
Aug. 23,	James D. Delvee,	23
Dec. 19,	A. Shepard Phillips,	14
" 22,	Mrs. Thomas Chase,	72
" 25,	Frederic Gale,	10
May	Joseph W. Sawyer,	19
July	James Henry Fuller,	22

1865.

Date	Name	Age
Jan. 27,	Joseph W. Ellis,	30
Feb. 20,	Eben. G. Ball, Esq.,	39
" 28,	David Ball,	85
Mar. 4,	Miss Eliza Shepard,	62
" 9,	George Cooper,	14
Apr. 7,	Harriet Goldsbury,	22
" 19,	Wid. Caleb Weeks,	84
" 28,	Dr. Amos Taylor,	80
May 4,	Wid. Jona. Moore,	76
Aug. 2,	Mrs. Calvin D. Shepardson,	41
" 8,	Sam. W. Goldsbury,	66
Sept. 1,	Ebenezer Goodwin,	35
" 25,	Wid. Samuel Ball,	90
Dec. 12,	Sam. G. Robbins, jun.,	30
" 22,	Wid. Peter Sandin,	82
" 27,	Luther Smith,	83

1866.

Date	Name	Age
Feb. 3,	Charles Johnson,	12
" 11,	Dau. of Stephen Johnson, 17 mos.	
Apr. 9,	Mr. Franklin Whitney,	46
May 11,	Mrs. Harriet Dill,	36
" 12,	Mrs. Esther Morton,	90
Aug. 5,	Wid. Simeon Stearns,	79
" 11,	Wid. Experience Fisk,	82
" 15,	Mrs. Nath. G. Stevens,	77
Oct. 4,	Mrs. Jona. Shepardson,	70

Date	Name	Age
Nov. 23,	Alexander Cooper,	43

1867.

Date	Name	Age
June 2,	Jasper Leland,	61
July 7,	Benjamin Conant,	92
Aug. 20,	Aaron Morse,	84
" 23,	Liberty Patridge,	91½
" 24,	William Ward,	68
Aug. 30,	Dea. Joseph Wilson,	81
Sept. 19,	Miss Tamar Pickering,	74

1868.

Date	Name	Age
Jan. 29,	Mrs. Henry Atwood,	40
" 30,	Isaac Hastings,	85
Feb. 18,	Nath. G. Stevens,	80
Mar. 6,	Miss Polly Gould,	77
Apr. 2,	Willard Forbes,	57
June 4,	Nathan C. Morse,	89
" 6,	Capt. Asaph Davis,	32
Aug. 15,	Mrs. Susie E. Davis,	26
" 16,	Dau. of A. & S. E. Davis, 10 days.	
Sept. 5,	Henry H. Manning,	24
" 12,	Rev. Roger C. Hatch,	84
Nov. 4,	Richard Weeks,	54

1869.

Date	Name	Age
Jan. 3,	Sam. Davis Wheaton,	53
May 1,	Horatio Holbrook,	63
" 4,	Dea. Joel Pierce,	78
Aug. 7,	Mrs. Susan D. Wilber,	37
" 10,	Widow Rhoda Barber,	82
Sept. 6,	Miss Fidelia Proctor,	22
Nov. 25,	Isaac Whittemore,	70
Dec. 5,	Mrs. Artemas Hawes,	55
" 11,	Wid. Richard Weeks,	50

1870.

Date	Name	Age
Mar. 13,	Miss Polly Conant,	78
Apr. 6,	Josiah Conant,	73
June 19,	Wid. Obadiah Bass,	84
July 10,	Miss Esther Stevens,	81
Aug. 16,	Wid. Joseph Delvee,	64
" 19,	Dea. Danford Tyler,	57
Oct. 5,	Thomas Chase,	80

Oct.	18, Geo. Wm. Barber,	24	Apr.	20, Wid. Joel Pierce,		77
"	30, Wid. Sam. Delvee,	72	May	13, Mrs. Tim. Moore,		55
Nov.	2, Mrs. John Grout,	26	June	19, Miss Jane E. Bass,		31
Dec.	5, Wid. Isaac Whittemore,	76	July	10, Russell Brown,		80
			"	14, Mrs Elisha Brown,		70
1871.			Aug.	1, Miss Jane Spencer,		65
Jan.	2, William L. Moore,	68	Sept.	24, Mrs. E. S. Greenleaf,		31
"	2, Mrs. Otis Conant,	43				
Feb.	13, Wid. Nancy Merryfield,	78	Oct.	4, David Atherton,		23
			Nov.	20, Willis W. Johnson,		26
"	15, James S. Wheeler,	55	1872.			
"	22, Jacob S. Rayner,	58	Feb	1, Daniel Pierce,		50
Mar.	7, Wid. Henry Harvey,	70	"	19, George Fisher,		48
"	31, Miss Esther Fuller,	69	Mar.	26, Amos O. Bridge,		57
Apr.	2, Wid. Rev. J. Shepardson,	88	Apr.	15, Mrs. Adeline Pond,		40
			"	17, J. Wilson Hastings,		22
"	18, Joshua S. Sanger,	73	May	15, Harvey Conant,		61

Whole number in 30 years, 504. Average age, 43¼, nearly. Number per annum, 16⅔. Number over 90 in 30 years, 10. Number over 80 in 30 years, 49. Number over 70 in 30 years, 70. Number over the age allotted to man, 129 : a large number, truly, — partly owing to a healthy climate, and partly to the fact that many of our young people remove from town.

Our town has been considered very healthy, as the location is away from any large bodies of water or swamps of any considerable size. Most of its territory is elevated to quite an extent ; the air is consequently pure and bracing ; diseases are few ; the people industrious, economical, intelligent, and happy.

As a reward for the above privileges and attainments, they are remarkably healthy, and live to an advanced age, enjoying themselves, and retaining their faculties, both of body and mind. We have now living in town four persons over ninety years of age: three of them are natives of the town ; the other has been a resident over sixty years.

There are fifteen between eighty and ninety, and twenty-seven between seventy and eighty, in a population of less than eight hundred inhabitants. Their names and ages may be found in the following columns:—

Names of Males.	Age.	Names of Females.	Age.
Phinehas Child (widower)	95	Sarah Leonard (widow)	94
Samuel Williams (w.)	91	Elizabeth Conant (w.)	91
Ebenezer Barber (w.)	81	Sally Morse (w.)	88
Edward Goddard (w.)	81	Hannah Stearns (w.)	85
Jonathan Shepardson (w.)	80	Rhoda Wheelock (w.)	84
Jesse Gould (single)	80	Elizabeth Ball (w.)	86
Henry Whipple (w.)	79	Mary Taylor (w.)	83
Gardner Conant (w.)	78	Martha Jennings (w.)	82
Rev. John Goldsbury	77	Mary Stevens (single)	82
Harmon Williams	76	Augusta Gale (w.)	82
James Goldsbury	75	Clarissa Gould	80
Ethan Cushing,	73	Sally Holman (w.)	79
Warren Atwood	73	Lydia Moore (w.)	78
Harry Grout	80	Melinda Reed (w.)	76
Ezekiel Ellis	80	Lydia Ball (w.)	75
Amory Gould	73	Tamerzon Ellis	73
Melzar Williams	71	Mary Ellis (s.)	72
Rev. Charles Farrar	70	Katharine Smith (w)	72
Dea. Edward Mayo	70	Lois Smith (w.)	73
Elisha Brown	70	Nancy Fisher (s.)	71
Jarvis Davis	70	Thamar Williams	72
Reuben G. Hammond	70	Lucy Atwood	70
		Polly Moore (w.)	70
Males	22	Clarissa Brown (w)	74
Females	24		
Total	46	Females	24

Aggregate ages, 3,585 years. Average age, a fraction under 78 years. Twenty-two males and twenty-four females, including all those that have nearly completed their seventieth year, this twentieth day of April, 1872.

A LIST OF NAMES

OF THE OWNERS OR OCCUPIERS OF HOUSES IN WARWICK IN 1798,
AS RETURNED BY THE ASSESSORS.

[Copied from the original in the Library of the New-England Historic-Genealogical Society, Boston, Mass.]

Atwood, Joshua
Ball, Jonas
Ball, Samuel, sen.
Ball, James
Ball, Samuel, jun.
Bancroft, William
Bancroft, Ebenezer
Barns, Abraham
Barnes, Lyman
Bass, Obadiah
Barber, Joseph
Barber, Zechariah
Bangs, Isaiah
Blake, Jonathan
Burnett, Henry
Burnett, William
Chase, Thomas
Champney, Humphrey A.
Champney, Jonathan A.
Cobb, William, jun.
Cook, Daniel
Conant, Asa
Conant, Benjamin
Conant, Benjamin, 2d
Dana, Joseph
Davis, Jonathan
Delvie, Jonathan
Delvie, Peter
Dike, William
Eddy, Abel
Estey, Jacob
Fisher, Israel

Fisher, Abijah
Fuller, Isaiah
Goldsbury, John
Goldsbury, James
Goodale, Joseph
Goodale, John
Gale, John
Gale, Jonathan
Gould, Thomas, sen.
Gould, Thomas, jun.
Hastings, Nathan
Hastings, Jonas
· Hazeltine, Benjamin
Hemenway, Asa
Holmes, Luther
Jennings, Joel
Kilton, James
Kilton, Enoch
Leonard, Moses
Leonard, Jonas
Leonard, Francis
Moses, Samuel
Miller, Samuel
Miller, Gilbert
Mayo, David
Mayo, Caleb
Moore, John
Moore, Jonathan
Moore, Mark
Morse, Samuel
Ormsbury, John
Packard, Jacob

Pennyman, Bunyan
Pennyman, Peter
Pomeroy, Josiah
Pond, Joseph
Pratt, John
Proctor, Peter
Rich, Jacob
Rich, Caleb
Reed, Samuel
Ripley, Peter
Robbins, Isaac
Simonds, Benjamin
Smith, Jonathan
Smith, Josiah
Smith, Abner
Stearns, Nathaniel
Stearns, Ebenezer
Stevens, Wilder
Stevens, Nathaniel G.

Stockwell, James
Stow, Thomas
Thayer, Asa
Town, Ephraim
Trull, Benjamin
Watts, Nicholas
Warrick, Jesse
Wescoat, Richard
Wescoat, Richard, jun.
Wheelock, Eleazer
Whitney, John
Whitney, Daniel
White, Solomon
White, Jacob
Whiting, John
Whiting, Lewis
Williams, Triphena
Williams, Nathaniel W.
Willson, John, jun.

WARWICK PUBLIC LIBRARY

Contained, Jan. 1, 1872, 610 volumes. The additions for the year were 454 volumes. The Trustees purchased 73 volumes. Donations were received as follows: —

	VOLS.
Rev. Preserved Smith	12
Mrs. Mary (Blake) Clap	221
Wm. B. Trask, Esq.	66
School District No. 7	62
Hon. Alvah Crocker	7
Town of Warwick	5
Rev. Henry H. Barber	2
Unitarian Association	3
Miss Dabney	2
Mrs. E. S. Sibley	1
	454 vols.

Whole number of volumes in the library, Jan. 1, 1873, 1,064.

INDEX.

A.

AGED PEOPLE, lists of, 198, 227.
Ager, Solomon, an early settler at " Flour Hill," 18
Agriculture, 149.
Appendix, 183.
Arlington, 15.
Ashuelot River, 19.
Athol, 15.

B.

BAPTISTS, article in the warrant concerning, 47; society incorporated, 91, 165; church in town, and ministers, account of, 165-168; ministers of that denomination who originated from Warwick, 168.
Barber, Deacon Hervey, one of the committee to have charge of the History of Warwick, 7; history of the town continued by him from 1854 to 1872, succeeding Hon. Jonathan Blake, 125; lectured on its history, Feb. 17, 1863, that day being the centennial anniversary of its incorporation, 130; his list of deaths in town, from 1847 to 1872, 221.
Bark, hemlock, 152.
Barley, 119.
Bassett, Rev Edward Barnard, installed pastor of Second Congregational Church, 164.
Bears, stories of, 22, 135; den, 123, 148.
Beech Hill, so named from its former large growth of beech timber, 17.
Bell, church, first in town, 115; new one from Ames's foundry, Springfield, 115; taken from the rebels at New Orleans, and brought to Warwick, lines composed on occasion of it, 192; a present from Col. McKim, 130.
Bennett, Samuel, 20, 21.
Bills, Rev. E. G., pastor of the Baptist Church, 167.
Black Brook, 20.
Black-lead, 122.
Blake, Jonathan, sen., 16, 159.
Blake, Hon. Jonathan, jun., early history of Warwick, written by him in 1831 and 1832, 3, 9, 176; read before the Lyceum, 4, 9; delegate to attend the convention to amend the Constitution of this Commonwealth, 104, 196; town clerk, select-

man, overseer of the poor, assessor, representative to the General Court, senator, county commissioner, justice of the peace, forty-two years surveyor of land, 176; brief memoir of, 175, 176; poetry of, 177-182.
Blake, Samuel, transcribed the history written by his brother, 5, 9; wrote a brief notice of him, 175, 176; first marriage of, 209.
Blanchard, Rev. E. H , ordained pastor of Second Congregational Church, 163.
Boot manufactory, men employed in, number of boots manufactured, amount of business in, 152.
Boundaries of the town, 15, 110.
Bounty, to encourage settlers, 22; increased to twenty pounds in 1749, 23; to thirty pounds, old tenor, or the value thereof in silver, 1751, 23; to volunteers, 131, 136.
Bowlder, of about a hundred tons weight, which can be rocked with a single hand, 149.
Bridge, Rev. Henry M., installed pastor of the Second Congregational Church, 163.
Brimstone, 121, 122.
Brook, the, 18.
Brushwoods, manufactured, 153.
Burnham, Rev. E. M., pastor of the Baptist Church, 166.
Burying-ground, laid out, 37; some bodies removed from thence to the present place of interment, 67; additions to the, 103; trees planted in, 110.

C.

CATAMOUNT killed, 22.
Cattle-shows, 150.
Cemetery, donations for the benefit of the, 140, 143.
Centenarian, 111; death of one, 135.
Centennial anniversary of the incorporation of the town, a lecture given at, by Deacon Hervey Barber, 130.
Chair stuff, 153.
Chestnut Hill, named for its chestnut-trees, 15, 17.
Child, Phinehas, ninety-fifth anniversary of the birth of, 173.
Church, First, pastors of, and preachers in, 157, 160, 161. (See Unitarian.)
Church, Second Congregational, formed, 116; pastors and supplies of, 163, 164; preachers of, originating from the town, 165.
Clap, Mrs. Mary Blake, donations of, for the improvement of the cemetery, thanks of the town to, for her gifts, 140, 143; donations of, to the First Church and Society, 162, 163.
Clark, Rev. George Faber, installed pastor of First Church, 160.
Climate, 111, 128.
Committee, on the History of Warwick, 7; appointed by the General Court to lay out original grants, 13; to find out the nearest route from Roxbury to this place, 22; to lay out a road to Pequeage, 24.
Committees chosen, 7, 13, 14, 16, 22, 24, 29, 32, 35, 37, 38, 48-51, 63, 64, 66, 67, 69, 76, 79, 81, 82, 84-87, 102, 108, 109, 114, 115, 126, 133, 137, 138, 140, 162.
Common, the, of ten acres, 29; lands, laid out into two divisions of seventy-five and sixty acres each, 32.
Constitution of the State, proposed amendments to, two, only, out of the fourteen presented were accepted by the town, 104; additional amendments to, acted on, 114, 116, 117, 125, 128-130.
Copperas, 121.

Cornet band, 154.
Cornwallis, anecdote in relation to the surrender of, 41.
County, separate, petitioned for, 66; of Hampshire, respecting a division of, 82, 83.
Court, General, grant from, in 1735, of four tracts of land, for townships, each six miles square, in the admission of settlers to said territory preference to be given to petitioners and descendants of officers and soldiers who served in the expedition to Canada in 1690, 12.

D.

DANIELS, Rev. E. D., pastor of the Baptist Church, 167.
Davenport, James, a relation of his concerning the British, and the soldiers of the Revolution, 41, 42.
Deaths from 1807 to 1845, 214-221; from 1847 to 1872, 221-226.
Delegate to amend the Constitution of Massachusetts, 104.
Delegates to the congress at Northampton, 45.
Democratic party formerly in the ascendency, a change since, 119.
Diseases, 111.
Districts, school, 86.
Dog-tax, discharged by one day's work on the highways for each dog, 86; for benefit of the library, 140.
Dudley, William, Esq., proprietor's clerk in 1736, 14.
Dysentery, malignant, 159.

E.

EARTH, red, 122.
Electors of President and Vice-President voted for, the first time, 80.
Embargo, memorial to the President of the United States for the repeal of the, 92, 93.
Episcopalian minister who originated from Warwick, 168.
Erving's Grant, 15.
Exports, 111.

F.

FAIRS, 150, 162.
Families or settlers, thirty-seven of them located on the first division of lots, 31.
Farms, 119; first ones of one hundred and fifty acres each, 17.
Farrar, Rev. C., pastor of the Baptist Church, 167.
Fay, Moses, had "Hobson's choice" of pews in meeting-house, 77.
Fay, Rev. L, pastor of the Baptist Church, 166.
Field farm, of four hundred acres, 16.
Fifty-acre lots, owners of in 1737, when the first plan of the township was made, also in 1761, and in 1872, 184, 185.
Fireplaces, old-fashioned, 21.
Firestone, 122.
Fisk Cemetery, 133, 134; soldiers' monument erected in, 146, 147.
Fitzwilliam, N.H., soldiers' monument made of granite from the quarry in, 147.
Flour hill, 17, 18, 173; why so called, 18.
Fort, the only one built in the town, 27; Lot, 27.
Franklin Glass Manufacturing Company, account of, 94-97.
Freestone, 122.
Fund for the support of Rev. Samuel Reed as minister, 80.
Funeral carriage, and a house for the same, provided, 82, 94, 109.
Funerals, public, of Lemuel Scott and Henry G. Mallard, 129.

G.

GALE, David, killed a catamount, 22.
Gallop, Samuel, petitions the General Court for land, in consideration of his services in the Canada expedition of 1690, 14.
Gardner, Capt. Andrew, in Canada expedition, 14.
Gardner's Canada, so called, now Warwick, 24.
Gilbert, Job, surveyor, laid out sixty-two lots of land, of over fourteen acres each, being the fifth and last division, 39.
Glass Company   (See Franklin.)
Goldsbury, Rev. John, 6; one of the committee to have charge of the history of the town, 7.
Goldsbury, Capt. John, representative to the General Court, instructions assigned him, 67, 68; chosen a justice of the peace, 70.
Gould, Thomas, had first choice in the pews of the then new meeting-house, 1786, 77.
Grace brook, 20.
Graves, Elder J. M., minister of the Baptist Church, 165.
Great farm, 16
Grist-mill, voted in 1759, to build one, and a committee chosen to select the spot for it, 28; built on Black brook, 31.
Groton, part of a leaf of an account-book found there, about sixty miles from Warwick, taken thence by the tornado, 107.
Grout, Howe, and Garfield carried into captivity, 26.
Guideposts, the first erected by law, 84.

H.

HAILSTORM, destructive one described, 170–173.
Hall, Dr. Ebenezer, originator of the Glass Manufacturing Company in town, 94.
Hastings, Miss Mary Ann, of Framingham, Mass., legacy of, to the First Church and Society, 163.
Hatch, Rev. Roger C., pastor of the Second Congregational Church, 163; death of, 163.
Hats, palm-leaf, manufactured, 111.
Hay, 119, 143; and other articles, the prices of, fixed by a committee of the town, 63.
Hearse, 82, 94, 109.
Hedge, Elisha, his donation, 87, 88.
Hedge, Rev. Lemuel, of the First Church, ordained, 28, 113; votes for his salary, 28, 29; liberty given him to lay out a hundred acres of land in one place, near the meeting-house, 29; answer to the call of the committee for settlement, 30; agreement with, for his salary, 35; difficulties with, 50, 51; death of, 62.
Highways, forty pounds raised to repair them, 36.
Hills, or high ridges of land, selected for the first settlements, 15.
Hix, Elder, his delusions and disgraceful exit from the town, 59–61.
Hodge, Elder Levi, pastor of the Baptist Church, 165; death of, 166.
Home lots, laid out, to contain not less than fifty, nor more than sixty acres, began to be numbered in the south-west part of the town, 14, 15.
Horses, the town voted three thousand one hundred pounds to pay for, for the Continental service, 65.
House, eighteen feet square, and seven feet stud, at the least, to be built by each settler or grantee, 13.

INDEX.   235

I.

INCORPORATION of the town, 132.
Indebtedness of the town, 129
Independence, national, the town votes unanimously for it, 54.
Indian capitivities, in 1755 and 1756, 26; corn, 119; mortars, 123; kettle, 148.
Inhabitants, general character of, 111; decreased, 119; more than one-twentieth of them seventy years of age and upwards, 227.
Instructions, from the town to their first representative in the General Assembly of the Province, 52, 53; to their representative in the General Court, 68.
Iron ore, 120-122; forge, 121.

J.

JARVIS, James, of Roxbury, first meeting of the proprietors of the township afterwards Warwick, held at the house of, in 1736, 14.
Johnson and his company, 16.
Jones, Nahum, 7; donor of land, 138; boot manufactory established by, 152.

K.

KELTON Corner, 20.
Kelton, Enoch, land-surveyor, 20; his wife confined fifty years to her bed, 20.
Kingsley, Rev. S. S., pastor of the Baptist church, 167.
Knob, Bennett's, 21.

L.

LAFAYETTE, shoes and stockings presented by him to our soldiers, 42.
Land sold at auction in 1761, for about four cents and three mills per acre, 32.
Lands, fifth and last division of, laid out, 38.
Langley, Capt. Samuel, agreement of, to build a new meeting-house, 71-75; his dwelling-house destroyed by fire, and the pews and doors, nearly finished, of the meeting-house were there consumed, 77.
Lawyer in town, 118, 192
Lead, 122.
Leather, 152.
Leonard, Moses, what is now the north part of the burying-ground given by him to the town, 67.
Leonard, Mrs. Sarah Blake, notice of, 164, 227.
Lesure, Mrs. Hannah, aged 101 years, anecdote and death of, 135.
Lesure, Samuel, sen., a soldier of the Revolution, 135.
Library, public, money appropriated for, 137; town voted to accept of it, 139; five trustees of, chosen, 140, 141; money appropriated for the enlargement of, 142; report of condition of, in 1872, 229.
Life, loss of, at tornado in Warwick in 1821, 106.
Light Infantry of the town, 125. 153; chartered, and officers of, 153.
Locke, Ebenezer, delays building a saw-mill through fear of Indian depredations, 25, 26.
Longevity, 111, 112, 124, 198, 199, 226, 227.
Lots, second division of, laid out in 1757, 16.
Lumber, 119, 151.

M.

McKim, Col., present of a bell from, 130.
Manufactures, 151.
Marriages and intentions of marriage, list of, from 1806 to 1844, 206-214.
Meeting-house, to be thirty-five feet long, and thirty wide, with nineteen-foot posts, 24; site for it first selected, 24; raised in 1756, in another place, 26; four pounds voted to enclose it, 27; standing uncovered two years after, 28; voted to finish it, 32, 35; agreement with Capt. Samuel Langley to build a new one, 71, 161; struck by lightning, 161; new one described, 115, 116; repairs on, 161-163; concerning it, 90, 91, 110, 115.
Members of the church, and worthy citizens of the old school, alluded to, 159.
Methodists, 112.
Military companies, two in town, a line established between them, 81.
Militia, 92; officers chosen, 47; enrolled, 129.
Mineral productions, 120, 148.
Minister, first settled, to have one share or a sixty-third part of the original township, 12; eighteen pounds raised to defray the charge of one on probation, 28.
Ministers in town, 112, 113, 157, 160, 161, 163-168.
Ministry, for the use of, one sixty-third part of the territory in the township, 12; lands sold, 81; in relation to the, 97, 101, 102.
Miry brook, 19.
Money, voted for Mr. Hedge's settlement in the ministry, 28; paper, depreciated, vote concerning, 56; voted to pay for horses used in the Continental service, 65; raised for town expenses, 118; to aid the families of volunteers, 130; expended on account of the war, 145, 146.
Monument, Soldiers', 145; a soldier killed at the raising of, 132.
Monuments, Stone, on the town lines, 129.
Morse's brook, 20; pond, 19, 20.
Mount Grace, so named from a child of Mrs. Rowlandson, buried near the foot of it, 19; its height, 123.

N.

Newall, Samuel, one of the petitioners for the territory (now Warwick), 12, 14; authorized by the General Court, in June, 1736, to call the first meeting of the proprietors, 14.
Noon houses and stables to be built on the meeting-house common if requested by the inhabitants, 79.

O.

Oats, 119.
Old fort, 27.
Orange, the town of, 16, 129; in part formed from Warwick, 67; district of (then South Warwick), joins with the town of Warwick in the choice of a representative to the General Court, 69.

P.

Packard, Jacob, chosen a delegate to attend a convention at Hatfield called to devise means to stay the Shays rebellion, in 1786, 71.
Padanaram, 19.
Pails, water, 152.
Paine, Esq., services at General Court in getting the town incorporated, 34.

INDEX. 237

Paper currency, depreciation of, 56, 62, 64.
Park, public, 137-139.
Party feelings strong, 88-90.
Pasture lands, 119.
Patriotic votes, and movements of the town, 41-47, 52-55, 58, 59.
Paupers, first mentioned, 36, 37; the inhabitants to keep them on town farm, 125-127; case, 128; expenses of, 134.
Peaked End, 19.
Pequeage, 15.
Perambulating the town lines, first record of, 79.
Petition to the General Court for town incorporation, 32; for a new county, 34, 66; for redress of grievances, 63.
Pews in the Unitarian meeting-house, owners of and prices, 116.
Physicians, 118, 192, 199, 203, 204.
Pierce, Daniel, donor to the Baptist Church, 167.
Poetry, 168, — by Hon. Jonathan Blake, Warwick, 177; Sunday-school celebration, 178; dedication-hymn for the new Unitarian Church in Warwick, 179; dedication-hymn, 180; lines to be sung at a donation party, 181; lines of condolence, 182.
Poetry by Elder John Shepardson, — reflections on the tornado of 1821, 188.
Poetry by Susie E. Barber, — the Rebel Bell, 190, 191.
Poetry by Miss M. A. Reed, — Hymn of Welcome, 205, 206.
Pomeroy, Lieut. Josiah, chosen delegate to attend a convention at Northampton, to state the prices of the necessaries of life, 63; Medad, Dr., 15; notice of, 204; lines repeated by him, 204.
Pomeroy's Pond, 19.
Population in 1860 and 1865, 132.
Postmasters, 199, 203.
Pound, to be built of wood, underpinned with stones, 84; new ones, 97, 114.
Powder-magazine to be built, 102.
Preachers, summary of those who originated from the town, 168.
Prohibition of the sale of ale, porter, and beer, 141.
Proprietors, meeting first held in Roxbury, Sept. 22, 1736, and after till 1761, 14; twenty shillings each, paid by the sixty, to defray the expense of laying out the home lots, 14; first meeting of, in the meeting-house, 30; last vote on record of, 40.
Province Land, now Royalston, 15.

R.

RAILROAD, the want of one, 120.
Rainstorms, 172, 173.
Rawson, Mrs Hannah, first town-school teacher, 38.
Recruits for the war, 131.
Reed, Abigail, report of a committee in favor of, 100, 101.
Reed, Rev. Samuel, the second minister of the town, ordained, 63; invited to become the Town's minister, instead of the Society's, 82; his answer accepting the invitation, 83; salary of, increased, 86; death of, 94.
Regimental orders, 186; men detached, 186, 187.
Report on the library, to be printed, 143.
Reports, 100, 101, 103, 126, 133, 134, 140, 142.

Representative, none chosen in 1783, on account of, as alleged, the extreme poverty of the town, 69.
Representatives chosen, 86, 87, 91, 192, 195, 196, 199.
Residents of Warwick over seventy years of age, 198, 227.
Rich, Lieut. Thomas, first representative from the town to meet the General Assembly of the Province at Watertown in 1776, 51; instructions to, 52, 53, 55
Roads, the first on record, laid out, 35; the first accepted, 36; important vote about, 39; seventy-six miles in town, all of them surveyed by Jonathan Blake, jun., 124.
Rock, shelving, of a large size, 148.
Rowlandson, Mrs., and her daughter Grace, 19.
Roxbury, or Gardner's Canada, now Warwick, 14.
Rye, 119.

S.

Salt, from Boston, for the inhabitants, 51; apportioned by General Court, 56.
Sawmill, in 1753, voted fifty pounds to build one, 24; delay in building it for fear of Indians, 25, 26; set a-going in 1759, 58; stood on Black Brook, 31.
Sawmills, 120, 151.
School, first, at the expense of the town, 37, 38; ten pounds voted to support it a part of the year, 37; Mrs. Hannah Rawson the teacher, 38; districts, first division of, 48; nine formed in the town, 69; defined anew, 114; bounded, 117; land sold, 81; money, 86; separated from the ministerial, 114; committee, 108, 200-202; select one, 156.
Schools, one of the sixty-three shares in the township, for the benefit of, 12.
Schools and schoolhouses, 86, 101, 102, 108, 128, 137, 142, 156.
Scott's brook, 20.
Scott, Samuel, his house to be fortified, 27.
Selectmen, 37, 193, 194, 196, 197, 199, 200; imprisoned, 78.
Settlers, original, to be admitted, to be sixty in number, and to have one share each, of the township, 12, 13; to be on the premises, to have a house eighteen feet square, and seven feet stud, and six acres of land brought to, 13; bonds required of, penalty twenty pounds, 13; estates to be forfeited to the Province within five years, in case of non-fulfilment of terms, 14; early, 124.
Severance farm, of two hundred acres, 16.
Sharp, Capt. Robert, moderator of the first meeting of the proprietors, 14.
Shays rebellion, 70.
Sheomet, Indian name of the surrounding country, 200.
Shepardson, Elder John, minister of the Baptist Church, 166; death of, 166.
Skunks Baron, 19.
Smith, Rev. Preserved, called to settle, 97; his answer, 98, 99; ordained, 99, 157; half-century discourse of, 158.
Soil, 111.
Soldiers, bounty paid to, for six months' service, 64, 65; and soldiers' families, money for the support of, 136, monument to, erected by the town, 146.
South Warwick, called the district of Orange, 69.
Spiritualism, 168.
Spooner, Samuel W., a delegate to the convention for amending the Constitution of the State, in 1853, 196.
State Constitution, non-acceptance of, 57, 64.
Stave and other mills, 152.

Stockings for the soldiers, knit by a centenarian, 136.
Straw-braiding, 111.
Strong, Caleb, voted for on the part of the town for County Register, 57.
Survey of the town, 124.

T.

TANNERY, 152.
Taylor, Dr. Amos, physician over forty years, 204.
Tileston, Thomas, of Dorchester, a petitioner for a tract of land for services in the Canada expedition of 1690, 12.
Tilton, Abraham, and others who served in the expedition to Canada, petitions General Court, in 1735, for land, which was granted, 12.
Timber on Town Farm to be disposed of, 137.
Tornado, a destructive one described, 104-108; lines concerning it, 188.
Town, meeting, the first, 33; plan made by Jonathan Blake, jun, 124; farm 126, 127; warrants posted, 128; officers, 132, 192; clerks, 193, 196, 202, 203; treasurer, 203.
Training-field, laid out, 29.
Trees, 119; set out in the burying-ground, 110.
Trustees of the Library, 140.
Tully brook, 20; river, 20.

U.

UNITARIAN Church, First Congregational, 157; plan of the interior of, with owners and prices of pews, 116.
Unitarian preachers originating from the town, 161.
Universalist Society, incorporated, 97, 118, 168; ministers of, and those who originated from the place, 168.

V.

Valuation of the town in 1860 and in 1865, 132.
Volunteers for the war, 131.
Vote, for numbering the people, 56; against adopting the constitution laid before the people, 57; to pay three years'-men in the service, 65; to raise men and beef for the army, 65.
Votes, patriotic ones, in 1774, 44.

W.

WAR of the rebellion, the town lost twenty-six men in, 132; their names inscribed on the Soldiers' Monument, 189; names of those from the town who entered it in the service of the country, 189.
War of 1812-14, men enlisted in, 185.
Warned out of town, all who were not inhabitants, 63.
Warwick, History of, read before Lyceum. 4, 9; committee on, 7; town of, appropriating money for the publication of, 8; territory of, one of four grants, each six miles square, granted by the General Court in 1735, each town laid out in sixty-three equal shares, one each for the first settled minister, the ministry, the schools and sixty settlers, 12-14; charges of laying out the township, and admitting settlers, defrayed by the Province, 13; first called Roxbury, or Gardner's Canada, 14; contained twenty-three thousand acres of land, exclusive of the Great Farm of sixteen hundred acres, and the Severance and the field farms, 16, 111; way from, to Northfield, 1740, Deacon Davis to mark it out, 23; town of, incorporated

Feb 17, 1763, 31; name of, probably originated from Warwick in England, or from Guy, Earl of Warwick, 33; first town-meeting in, 33; first town-officers chosen, 33, 34; names of owners or occupiers of houses in, in 1798, 228, 229.

Water of the town feeds three rivers, — Miller's, Ashuelot, and Connecticut, 124.

Way, public, marked out through Pequeage, now Athol, to Northfield, 23.

Wheat, 119.

Wildcats, thirty pounds bounty for killing them, 85.

Willard, Rev. William A P., ordained pastor of first church, 160.

Williams, Samuel, representative to the Provincial Congress at Concord, 46; at Cambridge, at Watertown, 49.

Wolves, voted to pay a bounty of twenty pounds per head on, 58; vote concerning, 64.

Wood, for fuel, 152.

ERRATUM. — Page 173, line 14 from top, *for* Flower Hill *read* Flour Hill.

www.ingramcontent.com/pod-product-compliance
Lightning Source LLC
Chambersburg PA
CBHW020805230426
43666CB00007B/871